TIBETAN VILLAGE COMMUNITIES

TIBETAN VILLAGE COMMUNITIES

Structure and Change

EVA K. DARGYAY

ARIS & PHILLIPS LTD
WARMINSTER – ENGLAND

© Eva K. Dargyay 1982. No part of this publication may be reproduced or transmitted by any means, electronic or mechanical, including photocopying, recording, or any information storage and retrieval system, without the permission in writing of the publisher. All rights reserved.

British Library Cataloguing in Publication Data

Dargyay, Eva K.
 Tibetan village communities. — (Central Asian studies)
 1. Villages — Tibet   2. Tibet — Rural conditions   3. Tibet — Social conditions
 I. Title
 951 5   HN733

ISBN 0 85668 151 2

Printed and Published by ARIS & PHILLIPS Ltd
Teddington House, Warminster, Wilts, England

CONTENTS

Acknowledgements		vii
Foreword		viii
I:	INTRODUCTION	1
II:	THE ENVIRONMENT	10
III:	DOMINANCE AND DEPENDENCY	16
IV:	THE SOCIAL STRATA AND THE RURAL SOCIETY	27
V:	THE FAMILY	33
VI:	GROUPS AND NORMS	49
VII:	THE ECONOMY	55
VIII:	THE POLITICAL STRUCTURE OF THE COUNTY	81
IX:	CHANGES MADE IN THE TRADITIONAL SOCIAL STRUCTURES OF TIBET BY THE PEOPLE'S REPUBLIC OF CHINA	83
SUMMARY		96
Notes		98
Appendix		103
Bibliography		107

LIST OF ILLUSTRATIONS

Plates

1.	A Tibetan Village near Gyantse	13
2.	Old woman in her traditional dress and ornaments, typical of the Gyantse area.	40
3.	Tibetan farmers at tea-break.	51
4.	Tibetan farmers with a plough that was in use until recent times	57
5.	When the cultivation of land starts the animals drawing the plough are decorated with ribbons and tassels.	63
6.	A Tibetan farmer harrowing with decorated draught animals.	71
7.	Domestic animals treading out grain on a threshing floor.	71

Maps and Plans   111

ACKNOWLEDGEMENTS

This study was made possible by the generous support of the Deutsche Forschungsgemeinschaft, Bonn, which enabled me to stay with Tibetan refugees in India and Switzerland long enough to complete my research. Furthermore I owe sincere thanks to Professor Dr. Dieter Schlingloff, head of the Institute of Indian and Iranian Studies, and to Professor Dr. Martin Bolte, head of the Institute of Sociology, both at the Ludwig-Maximilian University of Munich, who advised and encouraged me throughout my studies.

The publishers are to be credited for accepting the manuscript for publication and their help in making it presentable to the English speaking reader.

The Tibetans, commoners as well as members of the nobility and clergy, assisted me in carrying out this project. Without their sensitive help or their ready cooperation I would certainly have failed in my aim.

Last, but not least, I owe so much to the ever ready help of my husband, Lobsang Dargyay, who helped me to understand Tibetan culture better than any book I could have studied.

E.D.

FOREWORD

This book is based on interviews with Tibetan refugees in India and Switzerland between 1973 - 1979. The final manuscript was revised in 1979. Accordingly the most recent development in the relationship between the People's Republic of China and the Tibetans is not discussed.

After the Gang of Four was abolished being held responsible for every mischief and trouble that had occurred in Tibet, the situation in Tibet improved. Tibetans in exile may now visit their relatives in the Autonomous Region Tibet and letters are exchanged. Some Tibetan children from the Autonomous Region Tibet were sent to Dharamsala, the centre of the Tibetan refugees in India, in order to get a proper education. A liberalization with regard to the restricted practice of religion was announced in an effective propaganda campaign. The last step in this attempt was the publication of a highly priced volume with the sumptous title *Tibet*. Although it was published by Chinese authorities it was written by Tibetans who were apparently under the 'guidance' of the Chinese. Such collaboration is intended to indicate to the Western World that China treats Tibet as an equal partner with her own rights and characteristics.

Over the last three years the response of the West has changed concerning Chinese policy toward Tibet. The first journalists who were permitted to travel in Tibet were enthusiastic about the progress introduced by the Chinese; however, journalists who have travelled there during the last two years have noted shortcomings and failures of the Chinese system. Some of them had met Tibetans in Ladakh before travelling to Chinese occupied Tibet, and saw the differences in the faces and eyes of the Tibetans inside and outside of Tibet proper. Numerous reports, TV features, and photographs have revealed that most of the religious buildings are mere empty shells, beaming in the too bright colours of a new paint, indicating that the enchanting religious life of the Tibetans has vanished.

Various broadcasting companies of the Western World showed films of the fact-finding delegations sent to Tibet by the Dalai Lama. For the first time Tibetans had the chance to address a western public directly by means of modern technology. Mothers reported that they had to feed their children with their own blood — literally while young children deliberately made their prostrations in front of the delegation, imbedded in the spiritual aura of the Dalai Lama. Thousands of Tibetans, weeping for joy, exitement, and past grievances, stormed the platform on which members of the Dalai Lama's delegation were standing. The Chinese terminated the tenure of the delegation realizing that the situation had become uncontrollable. The world watched these scenes and became more sensitive.

Although the Chinese government has to enhance the present liberalization in Tibet and to return greater responsibility to the Tibetans, the difference between Tibet today and some other countries in South-East Asia should be recognized.

When we think of the situations in Laos or Cambodia we have to admit that the Tibetans are more fortunate.

Despite the fact that this book reflects data obtained some years ago, I believe that the general theme is as relevant today as it was at the beginning of the project, the results of which are now made accessible to the public.

Eva K. Dargyay
June 1982, Calgary.

I. INTRODUCTION

Changes in Tibetan Culture

Whenever the term "culture" is used in this study, it is to be understood in a socio-anthropological sense. Within this framework, culture is the total of man's behaviour which is expressed in different ways of thinking, feeling, and doing things, and is passed down from generation to generation. The ideas, as well as the behavioural heritage and its *objectification* as tools and implements, have undergone a change according to the situation of man's environment and his own instable nature. Thus, culture is the sum of human creativity in his striving to understand the world and make his living within it (Woessner 1971, 91). A change in culture occurs in the alteration of ideas and behaviour, in inventing and exploring. As to the swiftness of this change, one has to differentiate between evolution, which means a slow change, and revolution, which implies a speedy change, imposed and executed with force (Woessner 1971, 94).

As are all other human cultures, the Tibetan one was subject to change. Until now, only its periods of political history have been successfully determined, which are in turn the framework for its cultural development. These are the commonly accepted periods of Tibetan history:

Only a few sporadic surface finds from prehistoric times are available to the historian (Tucci 1973, 33). They are too rare to give any valid picture of this remote cultural period or its development. When the first mythical kings, cultural heroes, founded the Yar-lung dynasty, the basis was laid for the later Tibetan culture. The sources of this period list only the names of the newly established castles and the recently imported rituals and cults (Haarh 1969, 99-125). We learn from these texts names and facts, though we still are ignorant of the exact nature of change. This is also true of the historical period of this royal dynasty (7-9 century AD). The Tibetan tribes became unified under the reign of King gNam-ri-srong-btsan, a member of the Yar-lung dynasty. His son inherited an important empire and established political relations with the neighbouring countries: China, which had just become a significant power under the recent T'ang Dynasty, and India, which passed on to Tibet a considerable share of her rich and varied philosophical and religious thoughts. An alphabetical script based on some Indian script-forms was introduced into Tibet as well as Buddhism, together with its tradition and scriptures. China contributed several features of government management and administration, as well as much technical knowledge to the new Tibetan culture. The regrouping of social life can be traced: the hitherto powerful class of Bon-priests lost its influence and Buddhist monks and scholars replaced it. The old nobles, who regarded their king as a *primus inter pares*, now had to face a much stronger king, who knew how to use the new religion for his own political ambitions. Fraternal quarrels, murder, prosecution, banishment and usurpation are the visible marks of the internal struggle against these innovations brought about by the kings and their affiliated groups.

When during the ninth century, the power of the royal dynasty finally declined, Tibet became engulfed in a cultural lethargy, such as the few sources can only sketchily describe: The innovations of the preceding centuries seemed to dwindle away until, during the eleventh century AD., waves of new ideas swept once more across Tibet. At this time Buddhist scholars, travelling from India through Kashmir and Ladakh, entered Tibet, the Snow Land, and brought with them hitherto unknown Buddhist texts, commentaries, and a new understanding of the essentials of Buddhism. The rituals and instructions for a *vita comtemplativa* are not the main object of these studies, but those intellectual disciplines that contribute to the cultural heritage of Buddhism, i.e., logic, philosophy, the knowledge of disputation, poetry, medicine, astronomy and astrology. The ideas taught by Atīśa, who came to Tibet in 1042 AD, and by his Tibetan disciples, were elaborated and embodied into the Tibetan culture during the reign of the Sa-skya-pa hierarchs (1249-1358).

The nobility became so disorganised by its endless rivalries, which had started in the seventh century AD., that it remained unable to bring forth a leader capable of establishing a new dynasty and of putting an end to the quarrels that were aroused by separatist movements. The more alert noble families allied themselves with the heads of important monasteries and the hierarchs of religious schools or specific ritual traditions. At last the dGe-lugs-pa School, youngest of Tibetan Buddhist schools, was successful in the struggle for a new political system. Since the fifteenth century, this school has been headed by the Dalai Lama; although this specifically Mongolian title was not used until after the third Dalai Lama had been helpful to the Mongolian sovereign, his predecessors received this title posthumously, and in 1642 the Dalai Lama was installed as the king of Tibet. During the reign of the fifth Dalai Lama (1642-1682) the drive to establish a stable political system came to an end as did the process of assimilating elements of foreign culture that had begun in prehistoric times and attained its final state during the thirteenth century.

Since the eighteenth century, when Tibetan culture had seemed to stagnate (Stein 1972, 91), and the government concerned itself only with preventing foreign ideas and goods from penetrating the country, there had been no further innovations. This persistence in maintaining the *status quo* came to a dramatic end when the People's Republic of China invaded Tibet from 1950 to 1959 and brought about a radical change in all aspects of Tibetan life. Though handicapped by insufficient sources for the first half of the twentieth century, I was able to trace at least some new ideas in the field of Buddhist philosophy as well as in politics; yet the economic and social life of the people had remained almost untouched for two centuries. Thus we may speak of a cultural lag (König 1967a, 163).

This obvious stagnation within the Tibetan culture is an amazing phenomenon, which may be caused by a specific way of thinking involved in Buddhist philosophy.

Kamalaśīla (740-794), the well-known Indian Buddhist master, says in his *Bhāvanakrāma* (Tucci 1958, 242 7) that any disapproval of the Buddhadharma, the Buddhist doctrine, means to offend the Buddha himself. He quotes a passage from the *Sarvadharmasaṃgrahavaipulya* to support his opinion:

"Mañjuśrī, it is a subtle obstacle to refute the sublime doctrine! Mañjuśrī, such is the refutation of the noble doctrine: There are some who deem several of the pronouncements from the sermon of the Tathāgatas (i.e. Buddhas) to be proper and several others to be bad. He who refutes the noble doctrine insults the Tathāgata himself by refuting the noble doctrine".

Within the Tibetan cultural setting, this belief had a serious impact on everyday behaviour, as it was assumed that Buddhas were present in the world through their *sprul pa*, the incarnated Lamas, who usually shared their political power with some noble families. Thus to disapprove the actions of the government, to oppose the norms, or to promote new ideas, could always be considered "a refutation of the dharma". The risk of being discharged from an important rank and office, based only on a vague suspicion, did not encourage people to give way to new ideas and inventions. Within a totally different context, dPal-sprul Rin-po-che's report on the defeat of Nyag-sked A-mgo-rnam-rgyal suggests the same way of thinking, that is, looking at a worldly event from a spiritual point of view and seeing in it a mere sign pointing to a religious, metaphysical fact. Thus, in this report the bad king becomes a devil and his defeat is brought about by the protectors of religion (*chos skyong*) (Kaschewsky/Tsering 1973, 447-475). Even today a traditional Tibetan must not criticize any act initiated by the Dalai Lama, because he is the Bodhisattva Avalokiteśvara, whose essence is nothing other than compassion. Any step that might not fit very well into this scheme is attributed to the undeveloped mental capacity of the critic, who is not yet able to perceive the truth.

Despite these tendencies which hampered the development of Tibetan culture during recent centuries, when the pattern of Buddhist ideas was used to underline political power, there was some change. Due to the lack of almost any kind of archive records, accessible to the West, I can only give some hints indicating a cultural change. The Buddhist Tibetan literature was never concerned with "worldly" things, and as there was almost no secular literature, the sources for my task were few.

During the nineteenth century, scholars of the rNying-ma School of Tibetan Buddhism established the use of disputation and logical argument within their own tradition; these disciplines were, up to that time, studied by the dGe-lugs-pa and Sa-skya-pa only. By this move, the rNying-ma School became more attractive to intellectuals, as shown by the emergence of the *Ris med* movement that was to make a lasting impact on the spiritual and philosophical life in Tibet. Within the famous dGe-lugs monastic universities, such as 'Bras-spungs, Se-ra, and dGa'-ldan, a few scholars also followed this new way of thinking. Gene Smith (1970, 2ff) has given us a useful summary of this development, in which he clearly demonstrates the whole range of this intellectual movement. A further example of this kind of innovator is rDo-yul Shes-rab, a favourite of the XIII Dalai Lama, who tried to expound the Buddhist philosophy in a new way, based on his own reasoning and thinking. Though he failed - he had to ask for asylum in China - his disciple, dGe-'dun-chos-'phel, who was a monk of the 'Bras-spungs monastery, continued to pursue the aims of his teacher; he left the traditional ways of debating in the search for new ones. His philosophical treatises were prevented from being printed by the Tibetan government. He became involved in political rivalries and died, presumably about 1950, in Tibet.[1] Despite the ban on his treatises before 1950 they became wide-spread after 1959, when the Tibetans had left their country to seek asylum in India and abroad. By this turn of events his ideas influenced the thinking especially of the younger generation of Tibetan monk-scholars. dGe-'dun-chos-'phel showed once more, that the people of Amdo, to whom he belonged, strongly influenced the development of ideas on Tibetan culture.

During the first half of this century there were signs of serious changes in the field of politics, but they were never realized. Already the XIII Dalai Lama strove to curtail the privileges of the large monasteries, though he did not succeed in confiscating their estates. Under the prevailing circumstances this was rather a revolutionary step, and when the nobility and the high-ranking incarnations opposed it vigorously, the whole plan had to be dropped. His successor, the present Dalai Lama, also thought to continue these efforts but he was still too young to compete with the privileged groups. In his autobiography he says that it was his distinct aim to abolish the estates of the large monasteries and to reduce the power of the nobility (Dalai Lama 1962, 79, 83ff, and 99). The Chinese occupation of Tibet prevented him realizing his ideas, but there was also a new political awareness within some groups of the Tibetan people. In the eastern regions of Tibet, local chiefs and rich merchants asked for a reform of the whole political system. This move also spread to the capital, Lha-sa, and resulted in the establishment of the "Mi-mang" organization, i.e. "organization for democracy", which aimed to build up a democratic and non-communist Tibetan state (Peissel 1973, 142f). Some of the nobility also understood that time had come for a radical change; the former Minister of Finance, Tsepon Lung-shar, founded a liberal party, called the "Young Tibet Group" (Dawa Norbu 1974, 74). True, these movements and tendencies were of only limited scope but nevertheless, in Tibet, where people never used to challenge the political system, the ability to assimilate new ideas and to survive under new conditions was clearly alive.

In Tibet, new ideas were never given the bright light of publicity, but this does not imply that they did not exist. The more extensive our knowledge of Tibetan culture becomes, the sooner our initial concept of an almost paralysed culture will dwindle away, and we shall understand, that in Tibet, too, all cultural phenomena were in a constant process of being reshaped and rebuilt. Because of the preference for religion and philosophy in Tibet, new ideas were more easily realized in these disciplines than in other fields of human activity. For instance, as early as in the seventeenth century the Tibetans understood their myths of human origin to be stories told in a symbolic language indicating the historical development of mankind (Dargyay 1972, 175f), whereas western anthropologists only started to do so at the end of the last century.

Since 1950 the growth of cultural change had suddenly accelerated; new inventions, new theories about human life, new ideas and a foreign ideology that had never been heard of in former days, swiftly penetrated the whole country. Most Tibetans, especially the rural population and the older people, opposed this tendency, which was nevertheless forcibly promoted by the Chinese administration. This change was so radical, that people partly lost the feeling that the country, Tibet, was theirs. Along with the destruction of the traditional Tibetan culture, a lot of Tibetans felt like foreigners and became alienated from their surroundings. Thus, flight was the only way to escape, the only chance to uphold one's own cultural individuality. Tibetans who lived near the border, or were stout enough to undertake a dangerous journey, that would take months before they could reach freedom, sought asylum in Western-orientated Asian countries, or emigrated to Switzerland, the United States of America, or Canada. There, they at first tried to retain their traditional culture, but were soon confronted by the modern industrialized way of life, that they had never before encountered. Amazingly quick and alert, the Tibetans displayed the ability to absorb Western ideas and to incorporate them into the patterns of their native values. Thus, a people that till then had lived according to centuries-old traditions had to face Western civilisation of the twentieth century; the need for change became inevitable.

Socio-Anthropological Explorations within the Tibetan Region

Most of the few Westerners who were allowed to enter Tibet describe in their books among other things, and more or less at length, the social life, economic condition, and customs of the people. All this information was based upon casual impressions of the authors, who seldom were specialists in Tibetan Studies. Though these books give a lively and useful notion of old Tibet, they cannot substitute data gathered from social and anthropological investigations. Nevertheless, some of these books offer a lot of information, which would otherwise still be unknown to the scholars, as in, for instance, the books of Sir Charles Bell and his countryman, Sir H.E. Richardson.

As socio-anthropological explorations on a large scale proved to be impossible in Tibet, due partly to the xenophobia of the Tibetan government, and partly to restrictions imposed on the Tibetan government by Great Britain, Russia and China, anthropologists turned to the records of various persons who had travelled or lived in Tibet. P. Carrasco (1959) analysed most of the published reports and records and put them together to render a coherent pattern. He describes the actual situation of the country people and the different administrations in the main parts of Tibet. In the appendix he lists the relevant itineraries (op.cit. 283-295) and before starting the notes, he evaluates these various though secondary sources (op. cit. 229ff).

In 1959, when a representative section of the Tibetan people went to India to preserve their cultural integrity, socio-anthropological investigations of Tibetan groups could begin.[2] A good command of colloquial Tibetan, of the classical language of the Buddhist texts, and a good knowledge of the whole culture are indispensable for any research like this. The well-known British Tibetologist Snellgrove (1966, 199-219) had already pointed this out, when most Tibetologists were still unaware of the unique chance to enhance their understanding of the rural population in Tibet. He demonstrated with different examples how an anthropologist who does not know the native language fails to understand the natives' social behaviour, their norms, and the functioning of their institutions.[3] As the colloquial language is the only means of communicating with the Tibetan without being trapped in the boring misunderstanding arising from insufficient command of the language, it has to be stressed that the colloquial language is an important part of Tibetan Studies. Otherwise an anthropologist will never succeed in exploring Tibetan-speaking groups. Western Universities have recently started giving courses of colloquial Tibetan, and thus a few younger scholars have set out on this kind of research.

Among all the Tibetan regions the central provinces of gTsang and dBus were best known to

Europeans. At the beginning of our century British officials and explorers would set off from India to reach Lha-sa, the Tibetan capital, and thus they would pass through these two provinces leaving very useful records for us. Carrasco (1959) evaluated this material and put the data together to gain a coherent image of rural traditions, though until he began his studies he had never met a Tibetan. Melvyn Goldstein, an American anthropologist married to a Tibetan lady, was the first to interview Tibetan refugees in India. Most of his informants had come from gTsang and dBus. Since a relatively large amount of information on this area has become available to the western scholar further investigation is now possible. For this reason I was convinced that the best place to start my study of traditional village communities was a small area near the main route from India to Lha-sa. I happened to hear that there was a relatively large group of Tibetan refugees living in India and Switzerland who had come from three neighbouring villages in the district of Gyantse. From the noble landlord down to the shepherd, every kind of social strata was present, and thus I decided to focus my study on these three villages and their former inhabitants.

Without an adequate methodological background, however, I knew that I should fail in realizing this task. At this point I set out to enquire into the methodology of empirical sociology, and soon I recognized that the sociology of so-called "little communities"[4] offered valuable means for my purpose. To interview the people to be investigated, and to invite them to tell their lifestories are the main methods for gathering the data required for my study of the village-communities in Old Tibet, i.e. Tibet before the time of the Chinese take-over. Historical documents were also included in my research.

The "little community" is a unit small enough to show only one type, or a coherent set of several types, of the social and economic pattern and it is large enough to demonstrate the full range of social life and economical developments. To limit the investigation to one or two little communities, means not to become entangled in a variety of different types, and to avoid generalizations. This methodological approach would be of great advantage to Tibetan studies, hampered till today by an unspecific knowledge of the social and economic conditions that prevailed throughout traditional Tibet.

The smallest administrative unit was called in Tibetan *brgya tsho* which means "a county of a hundred [families]", although, in present times, the population of a "hundred-county" may well exceed that exact figure. One specific "hundred-county", as I shall call the *brgya tsho* henceforth, is the area of this investigation.

Aims and Plan of the Present Investigation

Till 1959 the "hundred-county" under investigation consisted of three hamlets; they were located on the banks of a river surrounded by mountains. This area is near the Himalayan border, and mainly for this reason a sufficient number of former inhabitants succeeded in arriving safely in India when the Chinese, after the occupation of Tibet, began purging all traditional elements, even within the poor tenants.

The period under investigation was limited by the span of a man's life-time. Most of the informants were in their forties or fifties when I interviewed them; thus they had left Tibet during their thirties or forties and their memories stretched over the period of approximately 1925 to 1959.

The most difficult task was evaluating all the information recorded on the social, economical, and political life within these three villages, as it was present during the last decades of Tibet's independence. As these recordings consist of the life-stories told by the former inhabitants they give only the view of an insider, and one expects, because of the flight and the many years that had elapsed since then, that in the speaker's memory the actual living conditions became a little more attractive than everyday life really was in former days. Thus the reconstructed picture of the traditional way of life will be based exclusively on the informant's memory; all marginal factors are missing, and no life-stories of wandering blacksmiths, beggars, or other persons who were outside the solid social structure of the village communities were available. Though I use the word "structure", I would not restrict the meaning of this term to a mere structuralistic sense (Levi-Strauss 1958; Oppitz 1975, 15 ff.).

In order to establish an atmosphere of mutual trust and faith, a close cooperation with the former upper classes, i.e. the nobles, proved to be necessary, otherwise there was a chance that most of the informants would suspect me of being a spy. Despite these restrictions the reconstructed scheme of former social and economic life in a Tibetan village community does not lack a certain amount of lively and counter-acting tensions. To avoid idealization due to the vague memory of the informants, I always asked for exact figures and amounts, etc., in order to get information as exact and precise as possible. This data was systematically analysed and evaluated, and, taking into consideration the inhabitants' own feeling about the former situation, I reconstructed the scheme of social, economic and political conditions important for understanding the lives of Tibetan peasantry.

The best way to undertake social-anthropological explorations is to go to the people that one wants to observe, and to start there with the research. Unfortunately, this has been hitherto impossible in Tibet; though some Westerners have been allowed to visit Tibet during recent years, the Chinese might not want to grant permission to a person who is well aware of the former cultural and social conditions and who could converse with the Tibetans in their own language. Furthermore, the aim of the present project was the evaluation of the traditional social and economic life. No-one would expect the Chinese to permit such research to be carried out in present Tibet. Thus, the only way remaining was for me to question the Tibetan refugees in India and abroad.

One of the main problems was to find people knowledgeable enough to provide valuable information and data. They also had to be former inhabitants of the "hundred-county" that was the target of the present exploration, and to have left their village only after they were fully mature and had participated in social activities. Anyone who fulfilled these prerequisites was asked for cooperation; most of them did their best to provide me with all aspects of their former lives. As almost half of the former population is now living in Switzerland and India, out of each social layer several informants were available. Later, this proved to be an advantage that enhanced the success of this investigation. All data recorded by one informant was verified by the report of a second informant who had to have participated in the same social and economic activities as the former. More than forty families were interviewed to get as much data as possible.

Of no less importance was the choice of suitable methods in order to obtain information. I am fully aware of the intricate situation of interviewing, involving both the interviewer as well as the interviewed person, and also of the inevitable subjectivity of every study on social life and common values, but I will not discuss these problems at length, because I assume that professional sociologists will make a better job of it (Myrdal 1969).

Except for members of the noble family who held an estate in this county none of the informants had ever been taught to think like scholars, so it was necessary to figure out a way of involving them in a form of communication through which I could learn what I needed, and they could participate in what was for them a normal feature of their world. Inviting the informants to tell their life-stories proved to be a good method, as the telling of one's life-story is a common practice among country people and is also an established genre of Tibetan literature (Vostrikov 1970, 180 ff).

In the field of empirical sociology this methodology is often applied if a case-study is intended. The life-story is a voluntarily communicated narration of all details of one's own life which should be arranged chronologically. The impact of the informant's surroundings on his own psychological development ought to be demonstrated, and the whole complexity of his environment seen through a "social microscope".[5]

In addressing an informant, I asked him about his life in traditional Tibet and about the conditions of his parents' lives. So stimulated, he started to tell his life-story. I did not interfere unless he neglected a point necessary for my investigation, or when his report seemed contradictory to me. To be sure that every aspect was included, I measured every life-story by an index of problems that I set up after my first communications with the inhabitants of this county. Throughout the investigation the same index of problems was applied; it ought to enlist all aspects of social, economic, and political life of the area under investigation. Each informant was asked to report only what he actually had perceived and experienced, and it became obvious that nobody was qualified to contribute valuable information outside the range of his own experience anyway. I recorded everything the informants told me on a tape-recorder; the essential passages of these records were translated and analysed, and I thus constructed an index of almost all the important points in their social and economic life.

It depended on the quality of an informant's narration as to whether I had to ask him a lot of questions or only a few. Whenever the report was vivid and decisive I never stopped the narrator by an additional question; this might destroy the whole atmosphere of telling a story. Thus, I presented my questions at the end of a passage. Some informants reviewed their lives in a cursory way, and their stories were full of cliches; I then tried to cross-examine the informant to make him discuss his life-story. This method is known as a non-structural interview.[6]

To formulate a question in a way understandable to a Tibetan farmer seemed at first to be an intricate task. As the Tibetan farmer is only used to answering questions that show an immediate application to his everyday life, all questions related to scholarly exploration seemed to be just verbiage to him. Hence I had to guide the informant step by step to the main question; an example will elucidate this: I was interested in how many rooms were in his parents' house. To put this question straight forward proved to be impossible, simply because it seemed to the Tibetan informant not to be related to the preceding question. Thus, I had to start with another question: "When you were a youngster, did you live together with your parents?" - "Yes, I did." - "Your parents stayed in this or that village, right?" - "Yes, of course." - "Did your parents own a house there?" - "Yes, certainly." - "And you lived together with them in this house - right?" - "Yes, our whole family lived there." - "Now, how many rooms were in this house? Do you remember, when you just entered the house, what was to your right and what was to your left?" Dependent on the informant's capacity and experience in abstract thinking I was compelled to dismember every question in this way.

This methodological approach consisting of life-stories and unstructured interviews enabled me to look at the social life of the group under investigation with the eyes of an insider. To evaluate the informants' actual feeling about their former living conditions and how these feelings were reflected by their thought processes seemed to me advantageous, though I recognise that this method also involved a serious disadvantage, as the social reality is mirrored only through the experiences of individuals who all belong to social groups that comply with the rules and customs of traditional Tibetan society. Aspects of social life that were considered by the informants to be unimportant, or which they were unaware of, were not told to the investigating scholar. One has to be aware that, in applying this methodology, to argue *ex silentio* is impermissible. Further, as the informants based their life-stories on their own memories, we might expect that most of the inconveniences of their former life had been forgotten during the years since they had to leave Tibet. To compete with the inadequacies of this method of questioning, I urged the informants to make their statements as precise as possible, to render measures and amounts instead of common considerations, and to rely exclusively on their own experience. Furthermore I compared this data with that contained in the books hitherto written on this subject, and with those given by other informants.

This study was further hampered by a lack of opportunity to quantify the records. The whole life of a Tibetan farmer was marked less by figures and quantifiable entities as in comparable times in Europe. Thus, most of the farmers interviewed found themselves unable to state exactly how many yaks, sheep or goats they owned; some even had seemingly forgotten how many children had been born to them, especially if they died shortly after birth. Throughout this study I present statistics only when they have been verified by the evidence of other informants; contradictory statements were put into the notes. I offer an average value where quantities differ from each other by small amounts.

Every scholar interviewing people or recording their life-stories will try to verify his reports. Commonly this is done by a special kind of questioning, which tries to entangle the informant in contradictions. This method never worked with the Tibetans; whenever I tried to re-affirm their former statements they replied "I have already referred to this item." In this case the only way of verification was to compare each statement with the statement made by another informant on the same subject. Serious divergencies that could not be settled in this way were presented to a group of three or four informants to discuss. Thus I got a valid perception of a full range of varying data.

Throughout my whole stay with the Tibetans, I never had the feeling that they wanted to cheat me or make me believe something. At the very beginning of my exploration I told them that it would not be reasonable to communicate only items they thought favourable to the Tibetan culture; this would make traditional Tibet look like a fairy-country. To show what traditional life was like in Tibet implies its unfavourable sides, too, and this was accepted by the informants.

During my stay with the Tibetans, I lived in the midst of them, sharing their everyday life and I was able to observe specific behaviour and include my impressions of it in this study. Furthermore, being married to a Tibetan who had been a member of the clergy in the former days of Tibet as well as being a Western educated scholar, interested in all anthropological and sociological issues, offered me an unique opportunity. I simultaneously behaved like a member of the Tibetan society, and analysed the particular situation with the training of an anthropologist. Within sociological literature this method is known as participating observation, the problem posed by applying this methodological approach as well as the "feedback" arising from the investigator's behaviour and affecting the group to be investigated are discussed in various sociological works. For this reason I will not dwell on this problem.

Tibet - a Promising Subject for Anthropological Studies

At the present time, when scholarly as well as public interest focuses on foreign cultures and questions how they handle the problems involved in mankind's social life, it becomes inevitable to investigate an Asian culture that remained almost untouched by the main currents that shattered Asian and European history during the last fourteen hundred years. Tibet was never conquered by the Huns, as happened to large parts of Europe during the 9th century; Tibet was never subdued by the Muslims, who overran all India and vast areas in Inner Asia, imposing their culture and ideas on the subjugated peoples. Tibet managed to remain on friendly terms with the Mongolian dynasty, established by Genghiz Khan, and to prevent the Mongolian army from penetrating into Tibet proper, and last but not least, Tibet has never been despoiled by the colonial ambitions of any European or Asian power. Thus, Tibet shows better than any other Asian country what the traditional life in some parts of Asia was like. Through being untouched by foreign cultural ambitions, Tibet displays a fully developed civilization with a specific script of her own, which has all the advantages of an alphabetical script unlike the script of her dominant neighbour to the East, China. Tibet developed a vast literature whose various branches remain even now partly unknown to the West; she established an important empire, reigned over by kings and priest-kings, that was for centuries a threat to all surrounding countries, including China and India; and Tibet evolved a very specific culture of her own, setting up norms and behaviour peculiar to herself. Though based on the Buddhist heritage provided by India, and to a lesser extent by China, the Buddhist philosophy in Tibet became an object for scrutiny, concerned thinking, and evaluation, so that Buddhist philosophy in Tibet did not merely adhere to Indian tradition but showed innovation in the traditional issues of Buddhism.

In Tibet, unlike China or India, Buddhism permeates, or more exactly permeated until 1959, all branches of cultural life, because of the historical situation. When Tibetan culture was still emerging from a variety of diverging factors, Buddhism along with many other cultural as well as social ideas was imported into the Snow Country, thus creating a unique and specifically Buddhist culture, that gave a lasting impact on vast Asian areas ranging from the Kalmuks in the steppes of South-Russia to the so-called Lamaistic enclaves in Peking and from Lake Baikal in Siberia to the subtropical regions of modern Nepal, Bhutan and other Himalayan countries.

Buddhism is well-known to be a religion very concerned with the lives of all beings, putting the "great compassion" (*mahākaruṇā*) in the midst of all practical endeavour and at the root of all spiritual development. Kamalaśīla, one of the eminent Indian preceptors of the Tibetans said at the beginning of his *Bhāvanākrama* (ed. by Tucci 1958, 229).

"The root for the whole Budda-reality consists in the 'great compassion' only".

It is reasonable therefore to ask what was the impact of Buddhism on the development of social structures in traditional Tibet, if there was any impact at all? Among others, this was one of the reasons that gave rise to the present investigation.

Later, impetus was given to this research-project by the political fate of Tibet in recent times. In 1959 when the Chinese army defeated the Tibetans who had opposed the dominance of these foreigners, the old economic system had come to its end; it was replaced with the harsh force of an administration that was not concerned with people but with ideologies. The social structure of former times still exists to some extent within the Tibetan refugee settlements in India and elsewhere, but we may expect the day when, under the stress of modern living, these survivals of a once impressive culture will have dwindled away. Thus, it is the duty of present Tibetan studies to document the traditional culture as far as possible while there are still people alive who are knowledgeable in the traditional customs. As the Tibetan refugees left their country more than twenty years ago, a considerable number of them are now old and will soon die. Therefore we cannot wait for better circumstances before studying Tibetan culture. It is still a living culture, but the old Tibetan culture could die out within a few decades as the cultures of the Mayas or Incas have, though I hope that this will not be the case.

The present study was first planned to be a case-study, but then it became apparent that a lot of conceptions turned up that are typical Tibetan, thus this study will contribute to our knowledge of the former living conditions, not only in the Gyantse district but elsewhere in Tibet. For instance the bonds that tie a tenant to his plot were the same throughout Tibet; the way of educating children, the way people tried to solve social conflicts - these were all very similar in most parts of Tibet. Though the period of investigation was limited to a few decades within this century, we may certainly assume that the life of rural people two or three hundred years ago was not very different.

II. THE ENVIRONMENT

The "Hundred-County" and its Villages

The area under investigation consisted of three hamlets or settlements, which together made up "a hundred-county", the smallest administrative entity. A certain number of these "hundred-counties" formed a district (*rdzong*, "castle"), which was administered by the *rDzong dpon* and by the Tibetan Government in Lha-sa (*bde ba gzhung*). The "hundred-county" investigated during this study belonged to the province of Gtsang, which the Tibetans call the "western province".

This county shared a lot of features in common with other counties elsewhere in Tibet. In one village the farmers were bound in duty to offer a certain percentage of their crops and dairy products to the Tibetan government, and had to transport government goods. As any kind of tax is in Tibetan called *khral*, the people obliged to provide the *khral* were called *khral pa* "tax-payers", and farmers obliged to pay the taxes to the Tibetan government were named *gzhung gi khral pa*, "governmental tax-payers" as I shall call them in future. The second settlement belonged to the tenants of a noble family who owned a large estate there, and the third settlement was occupied by the tenants of the monastery, which in its turn also owned some fields.

The population of these villages was classified into three categories that commonly made up Tibtan society, and most of the important classes were present therein – from the noble landlord down to the hired shepherd. Several professions were also presented, for instance that of the farmer, shepherd, craftman, head of the village, servant, etc. Near the villages there was an old Buddhist temple and a monastery with almost two hundred monks. In the middle of the county there lived a man whose duty was to protect the county from any damage by hail; he was called the "hail-preventer" (*ser bgag pa*). These villages were situated near the banks of a river, which was lined by a road. As this was the road used by government couriers, the villagers had constructed a small house to shelter them called the *kothi*, a word which is derived from Hindi but is much used in modern Tibetan.

This county was an entity in itself as it was independent not only in a socio-economic but also in a political sense. To separate a single village from this triad meant to mutilate a living organism. This becomes apparent only when all three sections of this county - the village of the governmental tax-payers with their grazing grounds, the estate with its tenants, and the monastic village with its tenants - are seen as parts of a single unit, related through their functions.

Most problems connected with this county and its inhabitants were settled by the administrative organs of the county itself. The *rDzong dpon* of Gyantse was the highest authority within the realm of his *rDzong*, his district. The noble and monastic subjects were to some extend excluded from this kind of self government, as some of the administration was done by the treasurers (*phyag mdzod*) of the estates.

For countless generations the inhabitants of this county had made their living there; they looked at their "hundred-county" as a continuing entity changing at such a slow pace that almost no one noticed it within his own lifetime. Therefore, the inhabitants lived together as a very intimate group; this is even true of the present exiles.

Let us now take a closer look at the district of Old Tibet in which these people lived. The "governmental tax-payers'" village, their grazing-ground, and the "hundred-county" bore the same name. Through the valley flowed a torrential river, which rushed down from mountains of almost 18,000 or 19,000 feet. The monastic tenants were settled a little further down stream among their fields. The village of the noble tenants crouched behind a rocky projection, in a bend of the river.

The barren slopes of the mountains overlooking the villages were partially covered with thorny underwood and dwarf-conifers. In the mountains, to the west of our county, there were some tiny settlements, but the country was uninhabited in the east. The mountain slopes could only be used as grazing grounds for the sheep.

The village population lived on the crops of their fields and the products of their herds of yaks and sheep. While all inhabitants owned small plots, some of them worked also as craftsmen.

The Houses

The villages were never surrounded by any wall or other protection. Without any apparent scheme clusters of houses were loosely spread over the whole area. The rich families' houses, large constructions of a rectangular shape, were isolated farm-houses, surrounded by the cottages and primitive dwellings of their tenants and labourers (*dud chung*). Sometimes the large farmhouse and the tenant's dwellings were constructed wall to wall, to provide more shelter from the icy winter-storm and to offer all inhabitants a common flat-roof, which was much appreciated as a sunny place for walking and talking. Occasionally the tenants' cottages, or two or three large farmhouses of "governmental taxpayers" were thus joined together to save building an outer wall. Nevertheless each house had its own entrance and separate living and storage rooms.

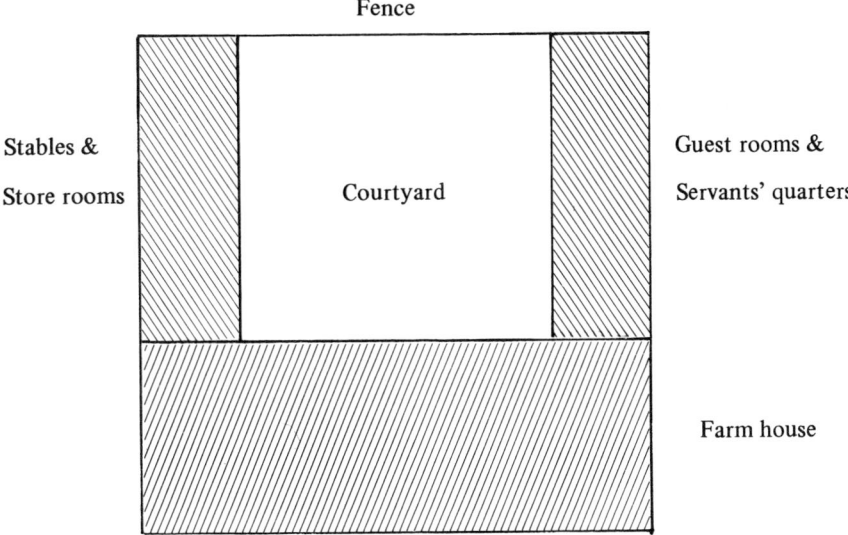

Fig. 1.   Plan of a Tibetan Farm

In all three villages, houses were constructed in the same manner, with stones, piled up and cemented with mud and clay; they were mostly two-storeyed, and the ground floor was used as a stable for cattle and horses. The ceiling was made by a simple wooden structure whose beams were overlaid with dry twigs, on which earth was spread and pounded into a solid layer. These houses were simple and lacked any decoration on the outside. The inside also offered only modest comfort, containing nothing but the ordinary household equipment. Wealthier families, as for instance the "treasurers" of the noble and monastic estates, furnished their homes with a touch of luxury. But even the homes of the "governmental tax-payers" could not compete with the decently furnished houses in Amdo, though they were not as austere as the houses of the other farmers.

The main farmhouse was a long rectangular building and on either of its ends a smaller and more primitive side-building connected it with the opposite side where a stone wall fenced in the whole property. The rooms within these two annexes housed servants and labourers as well as casual visitors, but also stables for horses and cattle were to be found there. Thus a spacious courtyard was formed by the buildings, with adequate space for all animals needed for transportation and riding. The top of the stone fence was covered by thorny scrub during the autumn, partly to prevent thieves from entering the property and partly to dry for fuel.

A new house was built when a young couple was unwilling or forbidden to stay with their parents (for further details on this rule refer to the chapter on Family). During the third Tibetan month (usually corresponding with the European May) people started to build houses, because the harsh winter prevented them from starting sooner. Everyone was anxious to finish a house before winter set in because the frost would make the walls crooked and full of cracks. When this proved to be impossible, the construction work stopped during the winter and was resumed in the spring. On average, two to five houses a year were built in the county.

To build a house, no special permission was required. The family commonly provided a young man or woman with a suitable site for their new home. Otherwise the young couple had to rent a plot. If the man wishing to build a house found a suitable site, he had to contact the "owner" of the land,[1] i.e. the person who owned the right to use this plot for farming or grazing. If the owner was a nobleman or a governmental tax-payer, then he might decide the matter for himself, but if the plot was owned by the community of the seven tax-paying families, then the village headman had to call the members of these families together to answer the request. Informants who had rented plots said that only a small amount of money had to be paid as rent to the owner of the land. Though this business is called in Tibetan usage *nyo ba*, which means "to buy", it was clearly a system of renting.

A wealthy family, intending to build a house, called for the *shing bzo ba*, the "wood labourer" to design and supervise the building works, which were carried on by a number of craftsmen according to the plan. The architect who lived in our "hundred-county", also acted as a carpenter and belonged to the category of monastic tenants. Today he is old and sick but, on my request, drew the floor plans of two houses which he had built before. Both houses were built for governmental tax-payers, i.e. for wealthy families. Unfortunately he did not agree to drawing the floor plans of a poor family's house.

Most families would design a house for themselves and would hire carpenters and masons to set up the essential parts of the house that the farmers could not build for themselves. If members of the family were trained as craftsmen they would not need hired workers. Rich families also needed painters (*lha bris pa*) and silver-smiths (*dngul bzo pa*) to decorate their houses. The common craftman earned five *bre* of barley a day which is about ten English pints.[2] The skilled men received a little more.

Now let us enter the house of a wealthy farmer. Before the family of a governmental tax-payer moved into this house, it had consisted of two main-floor rooms and a third room under the flat-roof. Afterwards the house was enlarged to six rooms. We enter the house (plan no. 1) through a small doorway, where a staircase leads up to the flat roof, but we keep to the main floor. Passing through a second door we enter a rectangular atrium decorated with murals, with a sky-light to allow the sun to penetrate the house in winter. These atria were popular social centres and were mainly to be found in the houses of governmental tax-payers. To our right is a guestroom and behind that the father's private room. Next to this is the family chapel, and above it an extra room to house the monks whenever they visit the family.

Opposite this part of the house to the left of the entrance, a door leads to the kitchen (*thab tshang*), the central room of the house, where the family usually gathers, and which is large enough to

Plate 1. A Tibetan village near Gyantse

accomodate the numerous servants and hired workers who also dine here. In the corner opposite the door, is the stove (*thab*) and to its right are the water jugs (it was apparently unusual for them to stand on the left). The family's stove is of a type called *rlung thab*, "air-stove", because the air is drawn from below. It is shaped like a staircase, with two or three steps. In the middle of the stove is a large pot and two smaller ones are placed higher up, on the steps. Fuel is stored nearby. In the centre of the kitchen a second fire-place (*dza la*) gives extra warmth on cold winter days. It is fuelled with peat bricks. Here, is the father's special seat with a small wooden table in front of it. The remaining members of the family sit on cushions along the walls. In the pantry next to the kitchen bags full of *Tsampa* are stored; and *chang*, a kind of Tibetan beer, and *'a-rag*, a kind of brandy, are produced in the brewery. Above it, a further pantry is used as a meat larder where in the winter months the air-dried meat (*sha skam po*) is produced. Near the entrance is a small toilet. It is merely a hole in the floor and of course contains no water. Because of the high altitude there is no odour, but sometimes ashes and sand are poured into the faecal pit.

Building plans of two houses drawn by a Tibetan architect are included in the appendix of this book. Each wall and every beam is included in the drawing as well as windows and staircases. According to our informants, the house of a poor family consisted of only one family room and two or three storage closets.

The walls of the houses, constructed of solid stones and about 1.50m thick, would stand to shelter many generations, though during recent decades they were not built as thick as in former days. If a house was badly made, decay might set in within a few years. Unlike Lha-sa and some other parts of Tibet, where the houses were whitewashed every year, in our county the custom did not exist. The houses looked grey and primitive because of the lack of any coating.

A strictly observed rule was that each family should inhabit its own house, which meant, that all couples of a lineal succession and their unmarried sisters and brothers, together with all their children and servants would occupy one house. In upper class families the father and his wife would sleep in a special room while the rest of the family slept in the kitchen. If the grandparents were still alive, they too would sleep in a room of their own. As long as the property was not passed on to a son or daughter, the young people preferred to sleep in the open air on the roof of the house

The children shared their mother's bed till they were weaned, when they moved into their father's bed. After some years they were given their own bed, but this only happened in the richer families, otherwise they usually slept in any suitable place.

An expanded family of several generations and with several couples living together in a single house was much admired. The role of each member was well defined so no instability or quarrel about rank and position was expected to arise. This problem will be evaluated in detail within the frame of the family structure in Chapter V.

Water Supply and Fuel

The whole area of our "hundred-county" had plenty of fresh water due to the numerous springs and tributaries of the main river. The use of each water course was exactly defined. Springs and brooks were used only for drinking and cooking, while the water from the river and its larger tributaries was used for field irrigation, for washing clothes, and for bathing. Usually there was a small brook near every farm house from which the servants fetched drinking water in large wooden tubs; so that there was no need to build wells as in Lha-sa. Only far-off farms needed wells, which were rectangular pits, with two-feet high walls above ground. The water was drawn out by a bucket on a leather strap.

People were careful to keep the water clean, not so much for hygienic reasons, which remained unknown to them, but for religious reasons, as it was supposed that snake-like demons, the kLu, resided in the water courses. By any pollution of the water they might become angry and hurt men with diseases. For this reason human faeces were never dumped into water courses.

As there was plenty of water, no law to regulate its use was required. Though I asked the former inhabitants several times, they kept on denying the existence of any kind of "water-right"; however we know very well, that such regulations did exist, at least, in other parts of Tibet. Carrasco (1959, 8) comments that plans of the whole channel system were filed by the district administration. In Ladakh irrigation goes back at least to the eleventh century, when it was said to have been introduced by the Indian Buddhist scholar-saint Atīśa (Bell 1928, 36). Within our "hundred-county" the community of governmental tax-payers as well as the tenants and tax-payers of the private landlords, i.e. the noble family and the monastery, were responsible for maintaining the wooden pipes and irrigation channels. If disagreement arose between two different landlords, then the *rdzong dpon* had to settle the quarrel, but it was the duty of the tax-payers to repair any damage to the irrigation system, whenever it happened on their property. It appears that in the hundred-county researched, no animosity had arisen between the different groups over the irrigation system for a long time.

Thorny scrubs and dwarf conifers growing on the steep slopes were collected by children, youths and servants for fuel. There were no restrictions on doing so. Dried manure of sheep, yak and cattle was commonly used as fuel and quite enough was available, though a family was only allowed to collect the manure of its own herds, or buy it from the herdsmen. These people, who were in charge of the numerous herds of the noble estates, collected the manure, dried and carried it down to the valley to be sold for their own profit. For details of this business refer to the chapter "Economy". Each of the three categories of subjects, had its own settlement area, its village. As shown in the map enclosed in the appendix, several families settled in an area pertaining to a category of subjects other than their own. This was usually due to some personal relationship or some other historical condition. As a common rule it may be stated that within a single village the large farm-houses of the tax-payers, governmental and private, acted as sub-centres around which the cottages of the hired workers, servants and tenants clustered, although some wealthy tenants (*dud chung*) owned remarkably nice houses.

The Tibetan village never offered such facilities as an inn, a town-hall, a dancing-hall or any other lasting social centre. All this had to take place within the private atmosphere of one's own house. People congregated for the most part in the large houses of the governmental tax-payers to discuss village affairs and drink a lot of *chang*, Tibetan beer. This system made it necessary for each person to keep his social life free from serious conflict unless he was to be cut off from social contact. Dances took place on the meadows near the village or, during winter, in the spacious farm courtyards.

III. DOMINANCE AND DEPENDENCY

Political Power

Since the seventeenth century the Dalai Lama has been the only secular and spiritual sovereign of the Tibetan people (Snellgrove/Richardson 1968, 195; Brauen 1974, 76). Every manifestation of political power originated from his person, and every kind of dominance over his subjects was based on him as the ultimate authority. Thus, he was, theoretically at least, the sole owner of the whole Tibetan country (Carrasco 1959, 28; Dalai Lama 1962, 84). The Dalai Lama's authority was not limited to a secular and mundane level, but was based on his supreme religious position. From the Tibetans' point of view he is the Bodhisattva Avalokiteśvara, essence of compassion, the mythical ancestor and protector of the Tibetan people. In this sense his position was and is above any discussion by Tibetans (Carrasco 1959, 80).

The Dalai Lama never exerted this power directly by himself; he delegated it to other persons, who then exercised political authority in his name, though often to their own use and profit. Passing power on to a single person or to a group of subjects is a well-established practice within the Tibetan political system. Those who actually exercised the power were also held responsible; to the prime potentate remained nothing but the fame and authority, and he found himself unable to interfere in the use of the power that originally had been delegated by him.[1]

Three groups shared the actual exercise of political power:
1. The central government in Lha-sa (*bde ba gzhung*) with all its officials;
2. The monasteries with estates granted by the government;
3. The nobility with its hereditary estates.

These three institutions exercised political power in a direct and active way. In a strict sense the central government was superior to the other two institutions, though in some cases their political power had already emerged before the central government existed; then the supremacy of the government was almost imperceptible, as was the case for instance in the Saskya principality (Casinelli-Ekvall 1969, 42). In reality these three power-exercising institutions were viewed by the Tibetans as being almost equal. Those realms of power which the Dalai Lama delegated to monasteries and the nobility might be confiscated at his request by government officials; this was seen as being the principal difference between the three institutions. To understand the village communities it is useless to study government organs or administrative bodies of monasteries and nobles, as these administrative units never came into contact with the average Tibetan farmer.

Though the three powerful institutions permeated the whole Tibetan state and country, the intensity and actual texture of their power showed some local variance, and it is therefore difficult to recognise a common pattern. The complicated pattern shown in the power and political supremacy of these three institutions is the result of a historical process lasting for several centuries. This process took place at a different pace in different areas, not as a unified, permeating movement, but as countless rivulets, that formed and established their own environment. The sum total of local privileges and investments made up the actual structure of political power. It was based on a pragmatic idea of the practical possibilities, including some moral aspects as uttered by "public opinion"[2], but was never founded on a judicial theory.

Those who exercised power in the name of the above mentioned institutions at the same time represented separatist movements, i.e. the nobles and the monk officials, who promoted the welfare of their own group. This, too, is an universal characteristic of Tibetan administrations. To entrust a person with power over his own group would enable him to remain close to the interests of that group and to neglect the superordinate affairs of the government. From the perspective of a *raison d'état* this is called a dysfunctional effect[3], however, the execution of power by members of one's own group (Wösner 1971, 99) resulted in less stress upon the subject and provided the whole social system with a stable base.

Power, in this traditional sphere of reference, is defined as the right to command manpower, and thus subjects were expected to submit taxes (*khral*) and service (*'u lag*) in exactly defined amounts. The command of manpower was essential in defining the practice of power. Manpower was never used for making profit as it is in Western dynamic economics, but only to sustain the economy in a very narrow and static sense (Aziz 1969, 158), that is, to provide all everyday needs. The nobles who were obliged to serve as officials in the government were invested with estates as a reward for their services. (Carrasco 1959, 96; Richardson 1962, 22; Brauen 1974, 135). The estates given by the government to monasteries were seen as contributions or donations towards maintaining the clergy or meeting the great costs of lengthy rituals. When a noble was endowed with an estate he was authorized to request service and taxes from the tenants living there. If the noble was invested with un-cultivated land, settlers were summoned by the government to become tenants of the newly established estate. Farmers and tenants together with their hired workers and herdsmen made up the population of rural communities whose social structure is now to be evaluated.

We might begin by asking who actually held power within the village communities. All groups that participated in the three powerful institutions and their control over land and manpower may together be called the governing class. Every rank within this class was recognizable through their particular clothing and jewellery (Dalai Lama 1962, 78; Richardson 1962, 15; Brauen 1974, 77f), but this ruling class did not have much impact on the rural population. The class of the subjects is called in Tibetan *mi ser*, which has been translated in various ways in Western languages.[4] When one observes the Tibetan usage of this word then it becomes clear that the term is best translated by the word "subject": the hired herdsmen was subject to his land-owning farmer, the tax-payer to his landlord, and the noble landlord was also a subject of the central government and the Dalai Lama, who was the only person in Tibet not to be called a *mi ser*. These arguments explain the preference for "subject" as a translation of the Tibetan term *mi ser*.

Special and unchangeable traits marked every subject who belonged to a specific landlord. Being born as a tenant or tax-payer under a landlord at once defined one's economic opportunities and the probable direction of one's further development. Belonging to a certain landlord was as decisive as being born into a particular family. As one was born into a particular family one was also the subject of a landlord. The sum total of a landlord's subjects formed a group of its own, clearly separated from the ruling classes. Within such a group a strong feeling of belonging together united all members. In social terminology this is called a "we-group" and we shall often meet this term in the course of our investigation.

The subject classes wore no distinctive clothing or symbols to indicate their social level, as was done by the ruling classes, the nobility. To belong to a certain subject-category was the only distinguishing mark within the rural population (Carrasco 1959, 28 and 86; Richardson 1962, 15).

The ruling class exerted power through their rank and reputation, initiating essential and decisive steps, which proved to be of great importance to the village inhabitants. The ruling class assessed the actual amount of tax and service, settled serious disputes, and inaugurated innovations of basic importance to the subjects (for instance whether or not to establish or close down a school). To a lesser extent the governmental tax-payers also participated in this decision making.

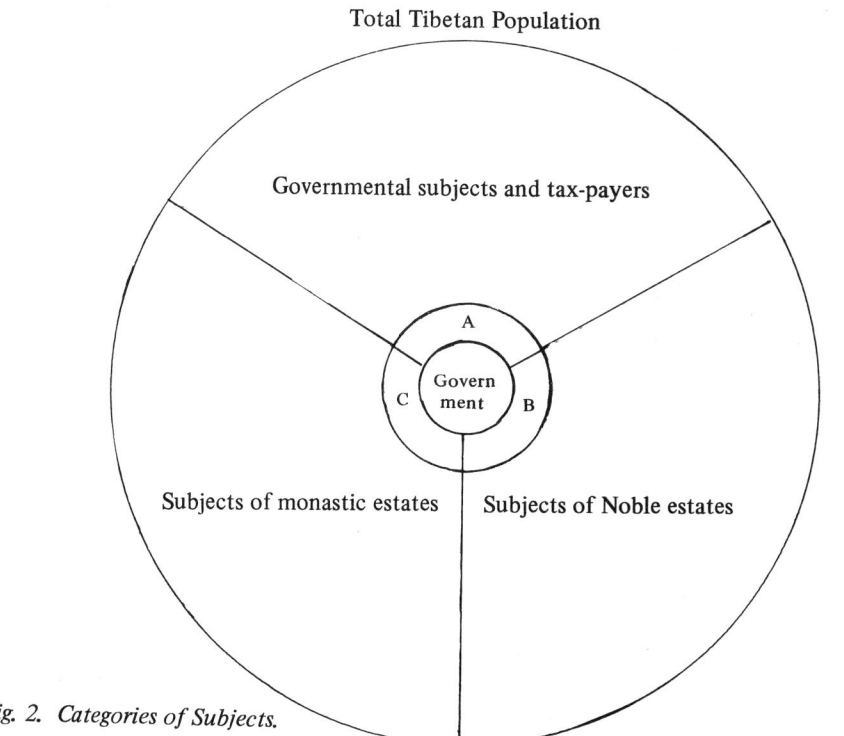

Fig. 2. *Categories of Subjects.*

A — District Governor
B — Noble Landlord
C — Monastic Landlord

Three Categories of Subjects

To the three power-exercising institutions corresponded the three categories of subjects:
1. The subjects of the central government *(gzhung rgyug khral pa)*
2. The subjects to the state monasteries (*chos gzhi'i mi ser*)
3. The subjects of the nobility (*sger ba'i mi ser*).

Every Tibetan belonged, usually by birth, to one of these three categories either as a ruling member, a power-exercising member, or as a ruled subject. Social sciences here apply the term "category", which signifies a large number of men sharing the same quality or mark, though not being connected by any individual, historical or biological process. Thus, the term "category" unites different peoples by quoting a specific item as their common mark and creates such statistic entities, such as for instance, "the smokers", "the pensioners", and so on (Johnson 1960, 48f). In this frame of reference we call the totality of all government tax-payers a subject-category, and the same holds valid for the subjects of the nobles and of the state-monasteries.

For instance a noble-subject from the Gyantse district may well never have met a noble-subject from the Phari district, though both belonged to the same category, i.e. to the noble subject-category (*sger ba'i mi ser*). Even when they met, they might never socially interact, though in the eyes of the Tibetan government these three subject-categories were the only institutions through which they could deal with the people, and levy taxes and services. Anyone who left his subject-category was considered a social drop-out, an outsider.

None of these categories was superior to the other; this is an essential difference from the "estates" in the social structure of the Middle Ages in Europe (Johnson 1960, 481), and is the reason why the social terminology of that time should not be used. In Tibet each subject-category was, according to its rank within the whole system, equal to the others, and comparably induced to pay taxes and to provide services for their landlord.

The ruling classes imposed a certain force[5] on the subjects in order to maintain the payment of taxes and did not allow them to become independent from their landlord (Bell 1928, 29; Carrasco 1959, 45 and 108). This step prevented fertile areas from becoming overpopulated which otherwise would have happened, had people been allowed to settle down wherever they wished. In Tibet, where it was always hard to till the ground, the government had to take steps to provide as large an agricultural area as possible, and to prevent the farmers from leaving their land. As there was always a serious lack of manpower (Bell 1928, 29; Richardson 1962, 16), it was imperative for the whole economic system to keep the farmers and farm workers on the farms and on the estates. Furthermore, the ruling classes could not impose too much stress on the tax-payers and tenants, or they would secretly leave the estates. A landlord whose tenants left the estate in an unusual way often earned a bad reputation, and this prevented new tenants from settling down. If, on the contrary, a landlord had a good reputation, as had the monastery in our "hundred-county", many new settlers moved there and became tenants.

The State of Dependency

Theoretically, the subject had to remain dependent upon his landlord throughout his life. As mentioned above, the state of dependency began at birth; within a single family it was inherited unilaterally: when the father was subjected to landlord A, all his sons would belong as tenants to landlord A, though the daughters followed their mother's dependency. Thus, among the members of each family, theoretically the male and female members belonged to different landlords. The tenant was incapable of cancelling the dependency during his lifetime, and the landlord, in turn, was not permitted to dismiss any tenant (Dalai Lama 1962, 84). Only the herdsmen became exempted from this regulation to some extent.

The custom of exogamy, i.e. marrying outside one's lineage, required methods for suspending the dependency. There were three methods of doing so:

1. To suspend the dependency, a "man-tax" usually had to be paid. This tax was called *mi bogs* by my informants, though in other Tibetan areas this term is used in a different sense.[6] On average, this tax amounted to some *srang*[7] a year and due to its extremely low rate was thought to be only a sign of respect, recognizing the supremacy of one's former landlord.

For instance, if a man intended to marry a woman and preferred to live at her home in a far-off village, he had to inform his landlord of his intention to ask for suspension of the dependency. Usually the landlords of the couple concerned would contact each other to settle the details. Paying the "man-tax" was the easiest way of suspending the state of dependence, but was only practical if the other brothers and sisters remained on their parent's farm to maintain the tax payments in the future. A single child was therefore not usually allowed to move to his or her spouse's residency, regardless of whether it was a man or a woman who intended to move. If this should happen, no one could inherit the farm, the soil would become fallow and the landlord would no longer be paid his taxes; so this had to be prevented. Thus, the single heir to a farm could only marry someone from far away and take up his or her residence there, if another relative or a friend replaced him, assuring that the taxes would still be paid.

2. A second way was to exchange two dependent tenants (*mi brje*): A woman, dependent on landlord A wants to marry a man, tenant of landlord B, and to live at his place of residence. If this woman moves from estate A to estate B, then landlord A has one labourer less. To avoid this, another woman has to move from estate B to estate A, commonly by marriage. To keep this system working smoothly, it was necessary that the duties of taxes and service be equal on both estates.

This was not the case of the noble estate in our specific "hundred-county"; the duties for taxes and service were extraordinarily heavy so that hardly anyone settled there voluntarily.

3. The rarest and most unusual way of getting rid of dependency was to become a free man. A subject might only apply for it for extraordinary reasons. First the supplicant had to find a mediator who stood in the favour of the landlord to submit his request while persuading the landlord to release the tenant from his dependency. Thus, the choice of the mediator had a serious effect on the result of the attempt. If the landlord finally agreed to the request, the supplicant paid a final fee of fifty *srang*. Within the investigated area no known person was freed by this procedure. - A popular case of gaining freedom was the later Tsarong. Born a tenant he managed to become secretary of the Tsarong family, a reputable noble family in Lha-sa. Eventually his landlord, the head of the Tsarong family, married him to one of the Tsarong daughters. On this occasion the tenant was given his freedom and adopted the family name of his previous landlord, i.e. Tsarong. For this reason English authors such as Bell and Richardson call him the late Tsarong, who rose from tenant to government minister. The whole story is told in a lively and sympathetic style by a former member of the noble family itself.

To summarize, the tenant inherited the dependency in a unilateral way from one of his parents. If an exogamous marriage was intended, three ways for transforming the active dependency into a latent and passive one were available: 1. paying the *mi bogs* tax, 2. exchanging two subjects relying on two different landlords, 3. freeing the dependent. Within this frame of reference we may speak of exogamous marriage when one married a partner belonging to another landlord, and intended to settle down there. Whether or not this partner belonged to the same subject category as oneself, remains irrelevant.

It was virtually impossible to free a whole family from dependency, though steps were provided for settling exceptional cases. Tibetan farmers and tenants very seldom sought their independence. Though they groaned at the taxload, they were disinclined to exchange their well-settled farmer life for that of the vagrants, who were infamous throughout the country. Every subject was afraid of being without the protection of a patron, which was the case when the dependency was cancelled. A farmer or a herdsman without a patron could not defend his own interests before the authorities, as for instance at the *rdzong dpon*, and so was without any protection from aggressive strangers. Furthermore, becoming independent usually involved abandoning one's house and fields, and leaving one's village, with all one's relatives and friends, and the prospect of being classified as a vagrant was most unattractive to say the least. The Tibetans considered the vagrants as "drop-outs", who were spoiled by vices unknown among decent farmers and herdsmen. In other words, the psychological chasm was so wide, that almost nobody wished to ask for a dismissal from the dependency. A Tibetan proverb, quoted by an informant, describes this situation clearly: "Above one's head a good house and a fertile soil to settle on" (*khang bzang mgo la g-yon / sa bzang gdan du btang*), nobody would throw that away!

A family intending to apply for freedom from dependency was assumed to have executed all duties painstakingly and to have no outstanding debts. As soon as it was learned that the family intended to leave the dependency everyone tried to make it change its mind. Friends and relatives inquired after its motives and tried to intervene. If the tenant family kept to its decision, then it had to petition its landlord for its release. The way this petition was handled differed widely between each subject-category. A description of the sequence in the handling of such a petition in the category of the noble tenants follows, because among this subject category there was still a small chance of achieving liberation.

The tenant directed his petition via the steward of the estate (*gzhis sdod pa*) to his landlord; who then handed it over to a committee of twenty persons guided by the steward. This committee recommended how to settle the petition, and – all informants agreed on this point – the landlord followed the decision reached which was then proclaimed and documented by his treasurer (*phyag mdzod*), while the steward filed the document. Theoretically the former tenant might stay in the village and enter service as a hired man (*dud chung*), but in fact this would only happen if the supplicant was severely hit by the loss of almost every member of his family, and thus was unable to meet the tax payments.

Simply to quit the job by running away was a common, though illegal way of gaining freedom. The family secretly packed up its goods in trunks and set out quietly at night. The village headman reported that his grandfather, also a headman had left his village in this way because he owed the government such a huge amount of tax that he could never have expected to pay them. A herdsman from the noble estate referred to two further families, tenants of this estate, who did the same. If the authorities had been notified of the new residence of the escapee, he legally should have been brought back, but this happened only rarely according to the village people. The law and its enforcement had a wide gap between them in reality.

Under some circumstances the subject's dependency might be suspended for a certain period of time. If a subject wanted to undertake a long pilgrimage or a commercial journey, he had to inform his landlord, and so long as he succeeded in engaging a substitute to fulfil all his duties, the subject might set out on his journey and stay abroad even several years.

The situation was handled in a similar way when a subject wished to join a monastic community. He was not allowed to enter the monastery unless the landlord agreed and drew up a document to confirm it. Usually the landlord granted such a request, because otherwise he might be thought to oppose religion, which was extremely unfavourable in Old Tibet. As long as the former subject or tenant belonged to the monastic community, though he might actually live at home, he was released from the dependency and its duties. Whether a youth preferred to join this or that particular monastery seemed to depend on custom and usage, as set rules could not be found in the data I collected, though in other areas they obviously did exist. If a monk resigned from the monastic life, the former document of release had to be repealed and his landlord assigned him a new rank. Due to their skill in reading and writing former monks were preferred as secretaries in the nobleman's household.

Category of Subjects and Group

Among the members of a particular category of subjects no institutionalized social interactions were maintained, which were usually limited to the group within the category. The group developed among the subjects of a certain landlord. At this point two different groups are to be considered, a large one centring upon a certain landlord, and a small one centring upon a certain estate of this landlord, who commonly owned several estates in different areas.

Within the group centring on the economic unity of a specific estate, the pattern of social interactions was very complicated. A segment of this locally bound group built up the primary group [8], which besides the family, was the group satisfying the individual's desire for emotion and life-feeling; the enormous impact of these primary groups on Tibetan society will be evaluated below. Though social interactions primarily occurred among the members of an economic unit bound to a certain locality, social interactions were also established between the members of two parallel groups each belonging to a different landlord and to a different subject-category. These contacts outside the group limitations were often of an intimate character, as for instance when the best friend belonged to the monastic estate, though the other was a subject of the noble estate.

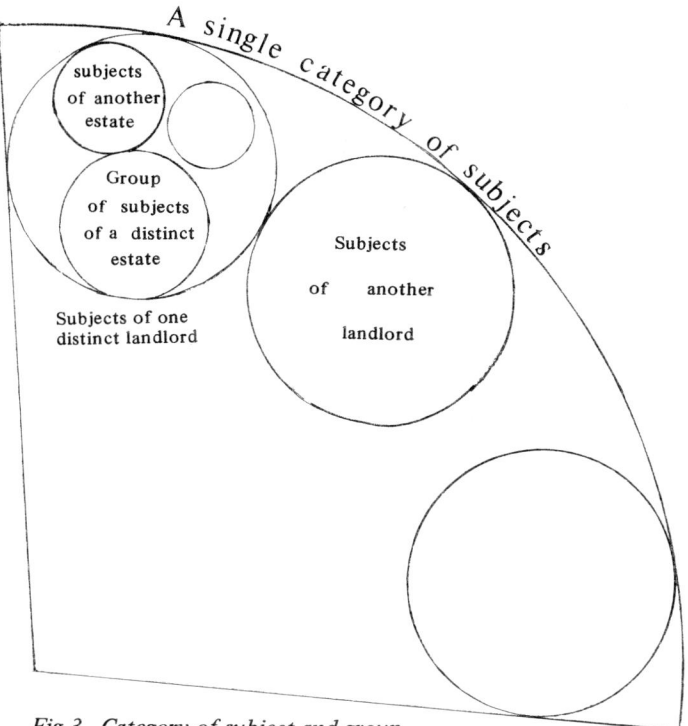

Fig 3. Category of subject and group

The subject-category was of basic importance for the state and its administration, though social life was realized on a smaller scale, centred on the economic entity. Within one hundred-county a handful of such groups existed, for instance, within the investigated area three such groups were discovered. The social interaction between these groups was rather limited to the upper stratas within them. Institutionalized interactions were limited to the managing and execution of public work (for details see chap. VII). The isolation of the economic groups is elucidated by the fact that each group separately celebrated the ploughing of the first furrow.

In summarizing the outlines of the social structure of traditional Tibet, Tibetan society may well be envisaged as a kind of "estate"-system, or as it is called in German "Ständesystem". As such it was more open and free than a caste system, but more limited than an open society.[9]

Characteristics of Individual Subject Categories

1. The "governmental tax-payers" (*gzhung rgyug khral pa*):

Within the borders of the investigated county there were seven families, equally ranked as governmental subjects and tax-payers. When a quarrel arose between the members of one of these families, it divided into two families, and since then eight such governmental tax-payer families had arisen. The original house and family-name remained the same for both branches of this divided family, but the syllable "*zur*" which means "side, margin" was added to the name of the split off branch.

When I asked the former inhabitants of these villages which subject category they thought the best, they unanimously answered "the governmental tax-payers". Most informants assumed that this category of subjects granted more freedom to its members. The term "freedom" has to be understood here only within the context of the informants' world. The governmental tax-payer thought himself to be free, as he decided every case concerning himself and the village among the village-council of the eight governmental tax-payer families. The duty to deliver taxes and service to the government or to its representative, the district governor, was imposed on the governmental tax-payers collectively, but the distribution of these duties to each family was the responsibility of the village-council, i.e. the eight families concerned. The governmental tax-payers managed their farms as they liked, no one interfered in their business. Hired men conducted the caravans which these tax-payers had to provide as government transport. The large amount of farmland owned by these families guaranteed them economic safety and made them feel "free", which was understood as not being under another's rule and not having problems of gaining a living. Furthermore, the village council passed decisions on any request for renting a plot of the common land. Many servants, hired men, and tenants depended on the governmental tax-payer, as they managed his household, tended his herds of sheep, goats, yaks, cows, and horses, and ploughed his fields, thus regarding him as their master. The eight governmental tax-payer families also chose two members from amongst themselves to act as village headman and his representative. This village-headman was responsible for the total county, which had the same name as the governmental subjects' village.

The prestige and responsibility which they held, tended to make the governmental tax-payers into a solid group, into almost a special cultural structure, or what is called a "subculture" by sociologists.[10] One became a governmental tax-payer only by birth, and the rank of a *khral pa* was passed on exclusively by male members of a family, that is by patrilinear inheritance. Along with his younger brothers, the eldest son received the farm and the social rank of his father, while the daughters were expected to marry and live with their husbands. If a governmental tax-payer only had daughters, a young man had to marry the eldest and live on her father's farm; he was called a *mag pa* and adopted his wife's family name (Taring 1970, 24). Though he participated in the prestige of this social strata, he and his sons could never attain the rank of a *gzhung rgyug khral pa*, a governmental tax-payer, but his daughters remained in this rank and thus continued the family.

The psychological and judicial ties that bound the governmental tax-payer to his soil were much stronger than in any other category. A governmental tax-payer could never legally leave his farm; though there was a rumour that some tax-payers had sold their farms, none of the informants could verify it.[11] The village headman's report that his grandfather had secretly left his farm to avoid paying taxes, is to some extent contradictory to the above statement. The highly esteemed rank of a governmental tax-payer and the favourable living conditions of this category of subjects prevented any wish to leave or sell the farm. Thus it was typical for the governmental tax-payers not to be able to understand the question, whether or not they were capable of permanently leaving their farm; they simply could not grasp the question, because the idea underlying what was asked was unimaginable to them. Especially for a governmental tax-payer, the surrender of his farm implied a serious drop in the social scale. Also, the district governor could never dismiss the tax-payer, though he might fail in his duty for a long period of time; only if the tax-payer was committed for murder might he lose his rank.[12]

It is mentioned above that the group of governmental tax-payers formed a cultural substructure of their own. Two features are remarkable: Among this group the prevailing marriage system was fraternal polyandry, and governmental tax-payers viewed this marriage system as being unique to themselves. Details will be given in the chapter on this topic. As all the brothers together inherited the farm and family goods, the economic situation as well as the number of farms within a certain county remained stable for long periods. This was another factor contributing to the social stability of Tibet.

The second feature marking this group of tax-payers was the Mani-brotherhood. This was the only group within the "hundred-county" established out of the free initiative of its members. The aim of this brotherhood was to cultivate the Mani-prayer. As the term "*maṇi*" denotes the Mantra *Oṃ maṇi padme hūṃ* by which the Bodhisattva of Compassion (Avalokiteśvara) is realized, the essential task of the brotherhood was to recite this Mantra, and thereby give the group a strongly religious character. A further function of this congregation was to celebrate the funeral of a dead governmental subject in a decent and impressive way. For this reason they collected donations to provide for the sacrificial goods and developed their own special funeral ritual.

The members of the Mani-brotherhood, all belonging to the tax-payer class, congregated regularly in the house of one or other of its members. Besides reciting the Mani prayer, they dedicated themselves to the drinking of huge amounts of *chang*, a beer-like alcoholic drink made from barley. All adults of the eight governmental tax-payer families participated in these meetings, and my informants amused themselves in describing how joyful these meetings had been. Only the steward of the noble estate was a non-governmental subject. The exclusivity of the brotherhood, the intimate meetings in the house of a "brother", the drinking of alcohol, and the regular ritual of these meetings, all gave the tax-payers a feeling of being different from the rest of the county population, who in turn admired the tax-payers for this exclusiveness.

The governmental tax-payers clung strictly to old traditions and showed a tough attitude towards criminals. For instance, when asked how they would treat certain criminals, who had belonged to their village and had now left prison, they replied that these criminals should be settled elsewhere, and never allowed to return to their former village. If the criminal had been a relative, a small amount of money would be given to him, but nevertheless he should leave his native area.

2. The Subjects of the Monastery-Estate (*chos gzhi'i mi ser*)

These subjects were divided into two sub-categories: the first, consisting of about one third of all monastery subjects, was bound to the monastery by indissoluble ties. This dependency was inherited by birth in the same unilateral way as already shown in considering the social pattern of the government tax-payers. Thus, the ancestors of the present-day monastery-subjects became dependent upon the monastery when it was first established. If it came to pass that a monastery-subject had run away and been discovered in his hiding place, he was, if necessary by force, brought back to the monastery-estate. There the escapee was punished with additional labour. On this estate flogging or paying fines were not customary. The second sub-category of monastery-subjects was recruited from people whose ancestors had voluntarily settled down as subjects and tenants of this monastery. Their economic condition and their social rank was equal to the first category, but differed insofar as they were free to cancel the dependency whenever they wished to do so.

Within our "hundred-county" the basic difference between the monastery subjects and the other two kinds of subjects was that only individuals were bound to the monastery estate and not whole families. Thus the amount of service requested was based on how many members of the family were subjected to the monastery estate.

Disregarding the category of the government subjects, the tenants and tax-payers of this monastery-estate were reputed to live comfortably, far better than the subjects of the nobility estate. This may be due to the high esteem in which religion as such and every thing connected with it was held, but also due to the prosperity and humanity of this particular monastic landlord. Only monastery-subjects stated they would prefer to return to their former living conditions, if this might be possible, while all others strictly denied this unrealistic suggestion.

It was remarkable that monastery-subjects who became criminals and were imprisoned at the district castle (*rdzong*) afterwards regained their former position. Usually they were employed as servants on the estate, being kept under better control and in less danger of going back to crime.

The monastery subjects lived under exactly the same conditions as the other subject categories; and I could not observe any pecularities resulting from their particular culture.

3. The Subjects of the Noble Estate (*sger ba'i mi ser*)

This category also had two minor subdivisions. The first was made up of the common subjects of nobility, who mostly lived as tenants on small plots. Whole families were bound by duty to the head of the noble family who was their landlord. The second group consisted of farmers who were subjected both as tax-payers to the central government and as tenants to the noble landlord. They owed service and taxes to both, but the amount of these assessments was lower than for subjects bound only to a single landlord, furthermore these subjects possessed large farms and employed several labourers so that they could easily afford the duties. The legal modalities of this mixed status were not explained in detail by any informant, though all assured me that there was a document settling all possible arguments; a copy of it was filed with the district governor as well as with the noble landlord. Due to this regulation they said that quarrels never arose.

This group of dual-tariffed tax-payers considered themselves superior to the common tenant and tax-payer of the noble landlord and a little lower than the government tax-payer on the social scale. The large amount of farmland that they owned, certainly fostered this feeling. When first addressed, these people claimed to be government subjects, and only after being plied with further questions as to why they were settled among the subjects of the noble landlord, did they concede that they were also the subjects of the noble family. The common subject of nobility belonged to the lowest strata within the tax-payers and tenants, and their fate was assumed to be the hardest. They reckoned that if a tenant harvested good crops through careful husbandry, then the landlord claimed a greater percentage; if a tenant's crops were poor, then he had to give away something from the little he had.

As a rule dependency was with birth, though within the category of nobility subjects as well as dual-tariffed tax-payers, a kind of social mobility was to be observed. Common tenants, if financially successful, could apply to the noble landlord for transfer to the group of dual-tariffed tax-payers, provided that they owned enough farmland and resources to deliver the various taxes of this group. The economic conditions of the dual-tariffed tax-payers were seemingly so attractive, that one of the stewards of the noble estate was eager to renounce his position for the status of a dual-tariffed tax-payer, though this actual move was prevented by the noble landlord. If he could not manage to till the large farmland and to deliver the various taxes, then a dual-tariffed tax-payer was demoted to the common subject and tenant status.

The actual amount of tax was related to the family as the only working economic unit, regardless of the number of members of such a family, thus, contrary to the system of the monastery subjects, the noble subjects were bound to their landlord in a collective way. The bond between the noble landlord and his subjects was of a certain paternalism which ought to be explained. The second son of the noble family lived in the nearest town and visited the estate and tenants at least once a year. The representative of the noble landlord, his treasurer, sometimes personally asked for certain services from the tenants. Above all, a single person, the noble landlord, head of his family, was earnestly concerned with getting as much as possible out of his estate. All tenants agreed that it was hard always to be ordered to do this or that by the treasurer (*phyag mdzod*) or by the steward (*gzhi sdod pa*). For these reasons all but one of the tenants of the noble estate were against returning to the old social and economic conditions. Nevertheless they thought of their landlord as a kind of father; this was indicated by using the word paternalism for describing the tie between noble landlord and his subjects.

Most of the nobility tenants were on very friendly terms with at least one person of the upper strata. This relationship of deep trust and faith enabled the friend, due to his higher position, to act as mediator between the tenants and the landlord.

A particular advantage of the noble landlord concerned was that he had established a school in the capital of the district, which was open to the children of the noble family as well as to the children of any tenant or servant family. All children attended the same classes, though the noble children sat on cushions, while the ordinary children sat down on the bare floor. No fees were levied, but if a tenant's son attended this school he was lost as a worker at home, so only a few well-off tenants could afford to send their sons to school.

If a tenant of the nobility who had been convicted of a crime and sent to prison, was now on the point of being released, the treasurer (*phyag mdzod*) came to the district governor in order to guarantee that the offender would now remain honest. For this reason former delinquents were employed as servants in the nobleman's household to fetch water, sweep the house etc., and were thus under permanent control; sometimes they were sent as shepherds high up into the mountain pastures, where they never had an opportunity to commit a crime.

Each of the three categories of subjects settled within its own area, which may be called a village. There was no indication that this separation of settlements was imposed on the subjects by any authority; it probably developed along with their economic situation. There were certainly several familes living in the villages of a different category of subject, mostly because of some personal or historic relationship. This way of forming different villlages for each subject category also implied that social contacts between the members of different subject categories were limited to the personal and coincidental. The subjects of the various categories might, when desired, intermarry, eat their meals together, visit each other, and have a member of another category of subjects as a best friend. These divided settlements were not like ghettos, as the members of the upper strata of these categories were united in the Mani-prayer-group.

The map attached at the end of this book shows the details of the different settlements. As the informants were not able to draw a map of their former villages by themselves, I drew it with their help and according to their corrections, thus, I present herewith the first outline of a Tibetan rural settlement, though this ought not to be viewed as geographically correct but as a structural scheme explaining the wider setting of the investigated area.

IV. THE SOCIAL STRATA OF THE RURAL SOCIETY

Till now whenever the strata of Tibetan society as a whole were discussed, usually stressing its hierarchical structure, the country people were envisaged as a solid almost homogeneous class (Richardson 1962, 15; Stein 1972, 99ff). The symbols of status, so typical of the gentry and high ranking clergy, were absent from the ranks of the rural population, and respectful language was unusual among the farmers, shepherds, and tenants. The differences between strata within the rural population were for this reason harder to point out, the boundaries were more vague, and personal aspects more important in creating one's position within the social scale in the country folk than among the gentry.

There were two basic means for evaluating social rank: 1. the ownership of land and herds, and 2. the amount of self-determination exercised by the family (Carrasco 1959, 28f). The main strata were easily defined: The stratum of the tax-payers (*khral pa*) and the stratum of the tenants and hired men (*dud chung*). Both strata existed within every subject category, but there were differences of number and significance. The government tax-payers usually owned large farms with plenty of land and herds; in return they had to pay certain tributes to the district governor. Those subjects who owed tribute service to monasteries and to noble families, who from now on shall be called "private tax-payers", possessed on average somewhat smaller farms than the government tax-payers. According to the French anthropologist Michael Peissel (1973, 86), governmental and private tax-payers owned together about fifty per cent of the whole of the cultivated land. The *dud chung*, the Tibetan term meaning "small family" (literally "small smoke"), held only small rented plots and some sheep and goats, and perhaps one or two yaks, *'bri* (the female *bos grunniens*) or cows; they owed no tax to the proprietor of their rented plot but they had to work as servants and farm-labourers on his farm during a fixed period every year. The members of this stratum could be summoned by their land-lord to execute this or that job within a certain amount of time. This outlines only roughly the strata, while additional and hitherto neglected characteristics will give a more detailed differentiation.

The families of the village headmen, due to their greater degree of self-determination and their leading position in deciding county affairs, constituted the elite of the upper class. All members of this class owned extensive landed properties. Within the other two categories of subjects the personal servants of the noble and monastic landlords replaced the village headman, however the governmental subjects did not consider them equal in rank and status to the village headman. It may be for this reason that personal servants, such as the treasurer and so on, belonged to the middle upper class. The lower stratum within the upper class was formed by the government tax-payers other than the village headman, and the stewards from the monastic and noble estate. The members of the lower upper class decided whether or not a newly arrived family might settle down in their hundred-county; if they did not let a plot to this family, it had to move on.

The middle class [1] consisted of the farmers of the monastic and noble estates. These farmers were called *khral pa* by the tenants who belonged also to the categories of the monastic and noble subjects, but the government tax-payers did not use the same word. This discord points out a difference between the government *khral pa* and the *khral pa* under a private landlord. The government *khral pa* had to deliver his taxes (*khral*) to the far-off district governor once a year; besides this stipulation he was a free man. In contrast the private *khral pa* owed service to his landlord; he had to till the landlord's soil and live near the mansion, always under the eyes of the treasurer and steward. This made the private *khral pa* feel that in spite of his relatively large farmland, though incomparable with that of the governmental tax-payers, he was never recognised as a real *khral pa* and lacked self-determination. Some private tax-payers owned large herds, some hundreds of yaks and *'bri* and thousands of sheep and goats as well as farmland. The herdsmen, though belonging to the private tax-payers, enjoyed more freedom and self-determination than the farmers, who lived near the administrative centre of the mansion.

The dual-tariffed tax-payers, who belonged to the government as well as to the noble landlord and owed tributary taxes to both, belonged to the middle class. Though they called themselves real *khral pa* and considered themselves equal to the government tax-payers, these for their part denied that the dual-tariffed tax-payers had the same rank and status as they. The dual-tariffed tax-payers held large farms and many yaks, *'bri*, sheep and goats, but due to heavy taxation they were not as independant as the government tax-payers. For this reason it is reasonable to place them in the middle class and not in the upper class as they themselves claimed. Unquestionably, the lower class consisted of tenants and hired men; here, too, subtle differences may be observed and lead to a more detailed social stratification. If a tenant or hired man was bound by duty to a government tax-payer, then he is in Tibetan called *dud chung*, a small family. Sometimes this term is also applied to the tenants of private tax-payers, but this is not correct. The labourers hired by a private tax-payer were called *g-yog po*, "servants". As a whole the class of tenants and servants was called **mo-hrang*.

The upper lower class was made up of tenants who rented a plot of fallow land from a government tax-payer. On part of this land the tenant would construct his house, while using the rest of the ground for agriculture. He paid his rent in cash which gave him a certain limited independence, which is clearly recognisable when compared with the rent by service, which shall be discussed below. Sometimes the tenant exercised another craft besides his farming. If he was skilled and if his craftsmanship was admired – as were, for instance, gold- and silversmithing – he could gain more social influence and a modest prosperity for his family.

The middle lower class is formed by those tenants who had to rent a plot of land in exchange for service. In both the upper and middle lower class distinct signs of this are found: a small plot of land rented from a tax-payer; no tax besides the rent; to sublet a part of his rented plot was impossible; lack of self-determination due to the poverty of these families, some of the family members had to work as servants or hired herdsmen.

The men hired, either as farmworkers or herdsmen, were the lowest of the lower class. They did not own any land that they could cultivate for their own benefit; they only had a few sheep or goats; economically they depended on hiring themselves out and thus lacked self-determination. Sometimes a son of a private tax-payer had to engage himself as a hired man to another tax-payer, for instance if for some reason there was a family quarrel, if the father was not inclined to hand down the farm to his son, or if the son preferred to remain a bachelor, separate from his married brothers.

Within this scale the ownership of agricultural land and herds as well as the self-determination decreases, while the right to move increases (Bell 1928, 29; Carrasco 1959, 108). Thus a hired man was subjected to another's command to a vast extent, but was legally allowed to travel, and while upper classes remained self-determined in all serious issues, they could not move from their estates.

Other persons, whose rank was not correlated to their property or self-determination, have to be included within the social scale presented here. Among these persons were the "hail-protectors" (*ser 'gag pa*), vagrant craftsmen, dance-groups, those who cut up dead bodies, (Tibetans disposed of the dead by cutting up the body and giving the flesh to vultures) and blacksmiths. The hail-protector was a member of the clergy, though married, and participated in its prestige; due to this circumstance he oversteps the limitations set up for our study of the rural people. His task was to protect the fields within the hundred-county from being damaged by hail and thunderstorms. After the last seed had been sown, he also acted as intermediary between the villagers.

All the other professions listed belonged to the despised crafts. If such a low-cast person exhibited a decent character, he might be viewed as being equal to the low-class people. Such was the case of the man who, living in the village of government tax-payers, cut up dead bodies. If, on the other hand, a person exercising a despised craft came along as a vagrant, the established house-holders of the villages looked at him as not belonging to the rural people, even if they were in need of his craftmanship. He was supposed to be an outcast, to whom the norms of the society did not really apply.

THE SOCIAL STRATA OF RURAL SOCIETY

Stratum	Status	Tibetan name
Upper upper-class	Families of both village headmen	*rgan po* and *rgan chung*, both belonging to the *khral pa* group
Middle upper-class	Treasurers and stewards of the private estates	*phyag mdzod* and *gzhis sdod pa*
Lower upper-class	Government tax-paying subjects	*gzhung rgyug khral pa*
Upper middle-class	Dual-tariffed subjects under the district governor's and the noble landlord's authority	— —
Lower middle-class	Private tenants of the monastic and noble estate	*chos gzhi'i mi ser* and *sger ba'i mi ser*
Upper lower-class	Sharecroppers with a plot rented for money	*dud chung* or **mo hrang*
Middle lower-class	Sharecroppers with a plot rented for service	"
Lower lower-class	Hired workers without a plot	"

Landlord and Tenant

The relationship between landlord and tenant (Dargyay 1978, 65-83) was defined by prescriptive rights. Whether a common written law existed or not still remains unknown, but it is certain that any decision was based on custom.[2]

The tenant's role required that he painstakingly and honestly executed his service and offered his landlord due respect; the latter was rather exaggerated. A tenant, who was not too good at his work, but full of reverence for his landlord was probably never harshly treated by the latter, because he complied with the norms and rules of Tibetan society and in general people were certainly inclined to excused his insufficient performance. Showing respect to those assumed to be above oneself on the social scale was the usual practice of the inferior, who thus gained useful protection from arbitrary actions of the landlord and other superiors, as popular opinion was always ready to support the humble and respectful man. This was demonstrated by bowing one's body, drawing in one's breath noisily keeping the tip of one's tongue visible between the teeth; further every sentence uttered by the superior was acknowledged by *lags so*, "I am listening". Despite the variety of these postures they exhibit a solid pattern. To this behaviour belonged also the custom of calling one's landlord a sponsor (*sbyin bdag*). This Tibetan term corresponds to the Sanskrit term *dānapati*, which denotes "master of alms" and was applied to those laypeople who offered food, clothes, etc. to the Buddhist monks. In Tibet, where the Buddhist monks were never mendicants, this term was used for any kind of sponsor. Besides this semantic change the term implied that the person called *sbyin bdag* behaved in accordance with Buddhist ethics, its core being compassion towards all beings (*snying rje*).[3] If the landlord expected his tenant to execute his duties, he himself had to behave like a sponsor. This behavioural pattern limited the range of expression for each party: the tenant should never murmur in displeasure or burst out with rebellious remarks at any decision of his landlord, but had humbly to bring forward his supplication, which usually exaggerated his real needs. The landlord never forced the tenant to execute his duties beyond the usual limits without losing his prestige, thus he complied with the tenant's requests as much as necessary, but without compromising totally his own interests, in order to keep his image as a *dānapati*.

Only a single informant out of more than two hundred reported that he was once flogged by his landlord (Carrasco 1959, 108). This is his story: When he was a youth of about sixteen or eighteen, he had married the young daughter of an intimate friend of his landlord. His father-in-law and his noble landlord settled all details of the marriage contract and the youth looked forward to a future without major problems. Once, when there was a vast surplus of grain, the youth, who had been promoted to be steward of the estate, and his father-in-law sold the grain, which they assumed to be in accordance with the noble landlord's wishes. But when later in the year the tenants asked the landlord to lend them some grain and he was informed that all the grain had been sold he grew very angry and flogged the steward, who was then locked up in the barn. Soon afterwards the landlord's treasurer gave him some *chang*, a beer-like drink, that made him so drunk that he recognized nothing of his "prison", from which he was released the next morning. The father-in-law acted as mediator and the whole dispute was settled to everyone's satisfaction. The youth continued to work as steward, and he became famous for doing a good job.

The landlord was never able to drive out his tenant, however lazy the latter might be, nor could he refuse to rent him a plot of land. The single risk a tenant had to fear was that the landlord would lend him a plot of bad soil, where the harvest-yield would be below the average. The most unfertile fields were assigned by lot, on which occasion every tenant chanted prayers so that the gods might prevent the allotment of these unfertile fields to himself.

Although all villagers criticised the former system of three landlord-institutions, the various inadequacies, the small amount of self-determination, nobody complained of brutal actions by the landlord. Even the young steward who was flogged by his landlord said that he was treated decently later. Certainly, a few conflicts have been forgotten since living in exile in India or the west, so one must be careful not to conclude that the relationship between landlord and tenant was free of tensions. Within the investigated area obviously brutal treatment was avoided by the landlords just as the tenants refrained from any rebellious acts. Ch. Bell, a former British representative in Lha-sa, who was an expert in all affairs of Central Tibet, agrees with this observation.[4]

In evaluating the relationship between landlord and tenant, one has to be constantly reminded that all issues communicated here are based on reports by the persons affected, and exhibit for this reason an everyday experience of the judicial situation. This inside experience gives a totally different impression from that applied in judgements guided by the law. If anybody exhibited a deviant kind of behaviour common people usually paid no attention to it and even sometimes applauded it. We might expect that, according to the law, the situation of the tenants was not too favourable, yet everyday life put the Tibetans under less force than harsh nature would have done. The material communicated in this book is not conclusive enough to reconstruct the judicial situation in traditional Tibet.

Mobility

There were two opposing tendencies concerning mobility: the preference for a permanent residence with a respectable farm was challenged by the deeply rooted inclination for long and distant travel.

Naturally the rural people were less inclined to travel than other groups. Among the farmers, i.e. the tax-payers, a change of permanent residence was never observed, unless a move was required by marriage, though a temporary absence, even if it lasted for years, was in common use. Institutionalized travel which occurred in certain periods, as among the herdsmen in East Tibet, did not happen in the investigated area. Only the practice of exogamy instigated local or regional mobility to some extent. Those groups which displayed more mobility, as for instance the craftsmen, were commonly married to women from distant villages; while groups with less mobility, such as the government tax-payers, married women from their own hundred-county.

Some families of tenants and hired labourers had lived for generations within the boundaries of this hundred-county; they were called "common people" (*spyi mi*), and enjoyed a considerable prestige. Even if only the father belonged to the "common people" his children inherited this rank. They were always allowed to return to their village, whenever they wanted to even if they had stayed for years at other places. As long as they kept away from their village they had to pay the *mi bogs* to the village council of the governmental tax-payers.

Social mobility, i.e. to shift from one class to another, either superior or inferior, is within traditional societies not as common as in modern ones. In Tibetan culture the best way to climb up the social scale was to enter a monastery, where everybody was offered the opportunity of a high intellectual training. A family member who had become a monk enjoyed a special prestige, shared by the rest of his family. Among his family he turned out to be the person who set new standards, and stood out like a landmark. Despite the importance of the monastic career and its serious impact on Tibetan society it did not happen within rural society, and is for this reason outside the scope of this study.

Besides the clergy, the servants of highranking noblemen could expect opportunities for upward social mobility, if they were intelligent, hard-working, and in the favour of their landlord or patron. An example that actually occurred within our hundred-county demonstrates this. A son of the noble landlord's treasurer (*phyag mdzod*) was remarkable for his intelligence and assiduity. He went to school with sons of the landlord and later on to the administrative academy (Brauen 1974, 138) in Lha-sa. After the final examination he was admitted to the civil service and soon attained the position of "Great Secretary" (*drung yig chen mo*), so becoming one of the four members constituting the Monastery Council, an administrative board of great influence at a very high governmental level (Richardson 1962, 23). In filling this position he was superior to his former landlord and his sons; the dependency was dissolved during the career of the treasurer's son, though his father and brothers remained in their former social status. A similar case was the career of the former defence minister Tsarong (Taring 1970, 18-21 and 24-26).

Within the rural society of our county, the chance for an upward social climb was extremely limited, if not impossible. Exercising certain knowledge and skill, as for instance calligraphy, reading or painting, promoted the prestige of an individual but it never enabled him to transcend his own class limits. One former tenant of the noble landlord did succeed in ascending from the lower to the middle class. This is, in short, his story:

When he was still a young man he left his family because of a harsh dispute. Together with his wife he built a new, but very modest home for his small family. Besides fulfilling his duties as tenant he hired himself out as a "tax help" (*khral skyor*) to his neighbours. Over the course of years he became a man of reputation and of some fortune, thus he met the prerequisite for managing a larger farm. Supported by his landlord, he joined the class of dual-tariffed tax-payers. This was a unique step, though open to all who were ready to work as hard as this man did; this was the only case of upward social mobility discovered during this investigation. Usually an ascension of the social scale was envisaged as happening through marrying a woman who belonged to the upper classes; for this reason the daughters of the government tax-payers were well appreciated brides. Several couples reflected this method of making a career.

Social mobility can also mean descending the social ladder; here, too, only a single instance was related. The eldest son of a private tax-payer (i.e. a *sger ba'i mi ser*) was not appointed as the heir of the farm but sent to the mountains to tend the sheep. There he remained till he left Tibet in 1959. Thus was this man degraded from being heir of a considerable farm to a mere shepherd, an employment thought in traditional Tibet to be the last job requiring skill and endeavour. Obviously this man was incapable of managing a farm on his own.

V. THE FAMILY

Different Structures

Within the three villages of our county two different family structures existed side by side:[1] the extended family[2], which is called in Tibetan "large family" (*mi tshang che ba*), and the nuclear family[3], in Tibetan "small family" (*mi tshang chung ngu*). Both types were associated with specific economic systems and certain subject categories.

Whether or not the family lived as an extended family or just as a nuclear family, the Tibetan ideal was that of three generations living together in one household. When I asked the villagers who actually lived together with their parents and their already married children, apparently almost half of all families were in disagreement with the above mentioned ideal. In most cases severe quarrels had disrupted the families. In families where a parent could not live with the eldest son there was always the option of moving in with a daughter, although she might be married and living somewhere else. When the second wife of the father and his son or daughter did not understand each other, the younger generation was sometimes forced to establish a new home for themselves.

The Polygamous Family:

The polygamous family was present in two different versions within the investigated area: as a fraternal polyandrous family and as a sororal polygynic family. The fraternal polyandry[4] had a great impact on the social system of the government tax-payers. Typically this family structure was always associated with large property, as one of the aims of this family structure was to keep the inherited farm as an economic entity and prevent it from being divided. Among the government tax-payers the polyandrous marriage system was unique; though some other Tibetan communities might have shared this custom, the majority apparently did not appreciate it very much. Nevertheless this structure of family provided a flourishing economic background to parts of the Tibetan society.

A family with many male members was appreciated in former Tibet, as the men were of much use in the hard work of agriculture and, furthermore, men could protect a family from attacks by robbers, thieves or unpleasant neighbours. Thus a family with many male members was founded on a strong economic base, as for instance, for the management of a medium-sized farm about ten adult family members were required.

Fraternal polyandry means that all brothers were married to the same wife, which in view of the above mentioned circumstances is a system that was obviously useful for the economic foundation of a family in Tibet.[5] During the marriage ceremonies all the brothers sat down in a line, dressed as bridegrooms, and all participated in the same manner in the ceremony. The brothers were equals in relationship to their common wife, though, in deciding family affairs, the eldest brother acted as the head of the family. The wife enjoyed considerable esteem and her main task was to create a mood of harmony and peace with her sexual contacts. If she succeeeded in doing so, the social reputation of this family was enormous, especially if three generations lived together in one household, which was, as already stated, the ideal standard.

As a rule these fraternal polyandrous families stayed in the village where the brothers were born and where their fathers lived; in short, these families were patrilocal, but not patrilineal. On the contrary the kinship was thought to be bilateral, that means that the relatives of all the fathers as well as the relatives of the mother were considered the common kinsmen of the parents and their children. Sometimes one of the brothers did not want to marry the common wife and looked for another of his own. If this second wife joined the polandrous household the polyandrous family became a group-family, but I could see that these group families were less stable than any other family structure.

A genuine fraternal polyandry only exists if all brothers participate in the marriage ceremony, and if all are dressed and behave like bridegrooms. Another form of polyandrous marriage is commonly confused with the one above described.

This second form of polyandrous family might be called a quasi-fraternal polyandry. At first it consists of a monogamous couple and after some time the brother, usually the younger one, establishes a casual sexual relationship with the wife; this kind of love affair was generally only due to the mutual desire of both.[6] The difference between the legal fraternal polyandry and the quasi-fraternal polyandry may seem insignificant to the outsider, but to the Tibetans it was essential: in the first case all brothers are husbands of the common wife and all are simultaneously fathers of all children, all brothers are involved in the process of deciding family affairs and in the second case only the eldest brother is husband and the father of all children; together with his wife he decides the family affairs, and if the younger brother disagrees with him, the younger has to leave. The Tibetans coined a special expression for this participating of the younger brother in the elder brother's wife, they literally called it "in this family is no disharmony" (Tib. *mi tshang 'dir 'khrug pa shor gyi ma red*). The formally unmarried younger brother lived for this reason in his brother's household. This type of quasi-fraternal polyandry was seen among the tenants, tax-payers, and stewards of both private estates, though most of these classes preferred monogamous marriage. Legal fraternal polyandry was not practised by subjects of the monastic and noble landlords.

Presumably this kind of quasi-fraternal-polyandry occurred among almost each class and group and was tolerated by public opinion everywhere. The Tibetans themselves did not think of this sexual relationship between the younger brother and his sister-in-law as a form of polyandry, and for this reason they habitually denied it, when asked whether theirs was a polyandrous marriage.

The circumstances which gave rise to this custom were obviously the often month-long absences of the husband, when he set out to barter and asked his younger brother to look after his family and household. When mutual love arose the younger brother and his sister-in-law would be emotionally bound together even after the husband's return.

In some families among the tenants and tax-payers of the noble estate, a sororal polygyny (Johnson 1960, 148, 151) was observable, which is when a man is married to two or three sisters simultaneously. The elder sister usually commanded a higher social position than her younger sisters. If a man married several wives from different families, all informants assured me that this would only lead to quarrels, because the different wives would not be used to living together and thus, unlike sisters born and brought up in the same family, jealousy would tear them apart. For this reason a non-sororal polygyny did not exist. On the whole, polygynic marriages were more rare than fraternal polyandry, but this may be valid only for the investigated area (Stein 1972, 96ff; Brauen 1974, 77).

The Monogamous Family:

The private tax-payers, tenants, craftsmen and hired men preferred by far the monogamous marriage in its nuclear type, where the couple lived together just with their children (Johnson 1960, 148ff, 155, 443). This family structure resulted from the economic situation of its practitioners: Their business induced them to move from their parents' home to a new one. Furthermore, the usage of monogamy was also conduced by structural characteristics; as the young men of these groups voluntarily married into families with large properties. A son of a tenant family was probably not considered as an appropriate *mag pa* by a wealthy family, so his only chance was to marry the second or third daughter of such a family and to rent a suitable plot from her parent. Another example: a tenant's son, who lived in the government subjects' village and worked as a silversmith, married the daughter of a governmental tax-payer and thus made his fortune.

Such a monogamous nuclear family could easily be enlarged by the parents of the husband or the wife coming to live with them and become an extended multi-generation family. Monogamous families tended to have smaller properties and herds. Some families exercised a craft in addition to farming. Fields and pastures were rented from the landlords or from the community of the government tax-payers (Hermanns 1949, 264; Stein 1972, 96ff; Brauen 1974, 80).

The Tibetan practice of marriage, as observed in the concerned hundred-county, shows characteristics which can be found throughout the world. The German sociologist R. König remarks in his voluminous "Handbuch" (1967b, 77) that the nuclear family occurs dominantly within the lower classes, while the extended family is more in use among the upper and middle classes, where properties and resources have to be handed down and preserved. Thus, he states, the different types of family occur in correlation to the social classes but it is not possible to assume a development from one type to the other because both types existed side by side in different classes.

The Family Residence

There were no common rules to decide where a young couple was to settle down (Johnson 1960, 153ff). The polyandrous families remained in the house of the brother-husbands' father or fathers, thus these families were patrilocal. If a family had only daughters, then the eldest daughter had to look for a *mag pa*, a husband, who was free to live with his wife and her family, so this young family was matrilocal. As far as I could see, this type of residence was extremely rare.[7] If heavy taxes and service were levied upon such a son-less family, no young man would want to join it; in which case the young couple preferred to pay the *mi bogs* to their landlords and settle down in a new place, i.e. a neolocal family was established. Only scarcity of women, apparently present throughout Tibet, may have resulted in the rare practice of matrilocal residence.

If a family was not forced into androgyny and the elder married son stayed at home with his parents, the younger brothers established new households as soon as they got married (neolocal residence). If the eldest son got involved in a dispute with his parents even he might leave the common household and set up a new one for his wife and children.

Roles and Ranks

The Head of the Family and the Wife's Role:

Within Tibetan culture the role of the head of the family was not as significant as in other Asian traditions. The husband, or the eldest of the brother-husbands in the fraternal polyandry, acted as head of the whole family. All informants cited the saying: "The head is the father, the mother is the base" (*gtso bo pha red/ 'a ma gzhi red*). The father's authority was based on his capability of fulfilling his role. If the father was disabled, his wife partially replaced him; in cases of severe sickness or death his wife might step in fully and take over the role of the family's head. In the case of the husband's death, the role of the family's head was never taken by his brother but always by his wife; only among fraternal polyandrous marriages did the younger brother replace the elder one and become head of the family.

The role of the family's head consisted mainly in representing the family's interests against those of outsiders and protecting it from attack. Within the family itself the power of its head was narrowly limited, as all family members, even the children, were involved in forming an opinion and in executing the decision.

The family head's authority was directly correlated to his education and character. If the wife overshadowed her husband in this point, then her word outweighed her husband's; the same was valid for older children, especially if they had been educated in a monastery. Both husband and wife held the power of disposing of the family property and wealth, though sometimes the remaining family members were involved in the decisions. As a rule the wife was in charge of storage, i.e. of agricultural products that widely replaced the use of money, and of the small amount of cash or gold possessed by the family. Without the wife's agreement the husband was unable to sell anything belonging to the family and vice versa. If the parents failed to agree, the other family members were summoned to discuss every point in detail. Most informants were of the opinion that the father would follow the wisest proposal so as not to be exposed to ridicule; others assumed that he would accept the majority's opinion, though respecting the minority's propositions. This method of settling a dispute derived, not from Western influence, but from an old tradition observed among the Buddhist monasteries in Tibet.

In the upper class the role of the family authority was more significant than in the middle class, while the lower class attributed only an inferior or almost negligible importance to the head of the family.

The evaluation of the mother's and wife's role is essential for understanding the Tibetan familial system. Commonly, women enjoyed much more freedom and prestige in Old Tibet than in other Asian countries.[8] Typically a Tibetan would mention his mother first, when asked about his parents. Wives' and mothers' high reputation and prestige, which may have been present in Tibetan culture from its very beginning, was fostered and promoted by the ideas of Mahāyāna-Buddhism. One particular form of meditation called the "Instruction on the sevenfold cause and fruit" (*rgyu 'bras man ngag bdun*)[9] especially trains the devotee to view all sentient beings as his own mother, thus making him concerned with rewarding them for their former kindness to him during his past unknown existences. As this meditation was taught predominantly to lay people, the impact on their emotions must have been considerable. Further, as women became a symbol for ultimate wisdom in Buddhist Vajrayāna, and as the prominent masters of Vajrayāna were supported in their spiritual striving towards enlightenment by a consecrated woman, who promoted her husband's spirituality, this tendency was much enlarged. The strictly ascetic and monastic ideas within Buddhism remained without any essential influence on the common people.

If a woman was educated and intelligent, she was appreciated by all classes, even more than her husband would be. In political discussions a woman's vote sometimes proved decisive, especially if she was competent.[10]

The village women were not as close to the exponents of religious life as the women of the nobility, though country women did give religion a prominent place within their families. It was the women's duty to offer butterlamps, water and incense at the household altar, unless a monk lived within her house (Bell 1928, 163f).

According to the opinion of the majority of the informants, the following qualities were desirable in a woman's character: to have compassion with all sentient beings and to benefit them, piety, a friendly and merry character, and diligence in managing household affairs. The upper classes added that she also had to know how to get on with servants and hired men. A reserved and demure temper was not favoured, and the ideals of Indian women were never approved by the Tibetans.[11]

Traditionally, a Tibetan woman enjoyed much freedom in the expression of her emotions; conjugal fidelity was esteemed for religious reasons,[12] but never strictly demanded. Jealousy was thought to be a failure, thus in the case of an extra-marital sexual relationship the jealous husband earned the scorn of the common people, but never the woman, who had fallen in love with another man. For the most part short-lived extra-marital affairs were never thought to be damaging to the marriage as such. This is elucidated by a Tibetan saying: "If a woman meets with another man, she won't suffer a loss" (*skye dman khyo ga gzhan dang 'phrad kyang zad 'gro dogs med*). For this reason a divorced or widowed woman might remarry without any difficulty; children, either legitimate or illegitimate, were never any obstacle.

Children and Youths:

Having children was natural (Bell 1928, 196ff; Ekvall 1968, 86f) and thus sterility was viewed as great misfortune. Around the children the family's emotions centred, all members and without exception loved and cuddled them.

When the child was still very small, up to about his or her fourth year, he was not held responsible for anything he did. If the child behaved in an inadmissible manner, the adults, not just the parents, diverted the child's attention to something else so that he would leave off his former behaviour. Small children were usually allowed to behave as they liked; the parents tried only to prevent them from causing any serious damage. All members of the household and also closely related neighbours spoiled the child, played with him, caressed and touched his skin as often as possible.

At about the fourth or fifth year the child was assumed to be old enough to assist in his parent's work. All informants emphasized that the main task in educating children was to show them how to work and how to use the various agricultural implements, and thus the children were constantly admonished to be busy and to execute the task as correctly as possible.

A child of seven or eight years old was viewed more as a small adult than as a child, and therefore children of that age decided whether or not they liked to go to school, to join a monastery, or to do something else. They participated in discussions of the family affairs and shared in the responsibility for the family's fortune.[13] Thus, a child of nine or ten years of age was fully integrated into the adult society. The individual character of the child was respected as far as it did not offend the social and moral norms.

Children wore the same clothes as the adults and shared their meals with them. Only small children had dresses of their own to teach them to be tidy, and they were fed by the adults, but not exclusively by the mother, who put dainty bits into the child's mouth. As soon as the children were physically capable of working they were involved in the working process of the farms. During leisure hours the adults sat down together with the children, drinking *chang*, playing dice, singing and dancing.

If a youth was distinguished by intelligence and character, his word and opinion was appreciated, even by elder people. He was made responsible for tasks which gained public repute, and he was encouraged to behave in accordance with the traditional pattern of values.

With this goal in mind, the young novices of the rNying-ma School were placed between elderly monks, and they were exhorted to guide the ceremonies by beating the huge drum, by intoning the prayers, etc. The youngsters felt themselves capable of performing their task very well, forgot the support given to them by the elderly monks, who in turn solicited more effort by applauding them. How exactly the children executed their tasks was not the main point of concern, which instead focussed on their willingness and strength to be submitted to the system acknowledged by society.

As the Tibetan youth was fully integrated with society, he was never in doubt about his status, unlike youths undergoing puberty in other cultural settings. Thus one could expect the Tibetan culture to lack specific rites marking maturity and no trace of boys' or men's fraternities. The youth's dress and costume was the same as of the adults, and his language was no different from theirs.

Today in exile, Tibetan youths imitate their Western friends and establish youth groups, mostly football clubs. Some of their members are not all all young, being married and already in their forties, which would have placed them among the grandpas according to traditional Tibetan thinking. Thus, even the so-called "youths' football clubs" do not exhibit the typical exclusiveness prevalent in such clubs of other cultures, and demonstrate, though in Western disguise, the old Tibetan custom of not needing any youths' fraternity.

If a youth decided to leave the common norms of his community, to abandon his specific tradition, this was tolerated; the youth was rarely subjected to any restriction. This is true, too, among Tibetan refugees in Western countries. Among the Tibetans in Switzerland I witnessed several times that while the father prayed aloud in front of his household altar, his son or daughter was listening to beat music just below. No one thought of opposing another's inclination or to show his displeasure. The long hair and modern dress of many Tibetan youths, although not appreciated by their parents' generation, is never severely disapproved of. Most parents are apparently proud of their children, since they have managed to survive in a world totally different from their former one, full of complications for the elder generation.

The date marking a youth's completion of maturity was only important for the tax system, because after that full taxes and service had to be paid by the former youth. This happened among the government tax-payers, when he reached his thirteenth or eighteenth year; among the tax-payers and tenants on the monastic and noble estate the duty for taxes and service started at a half rate at the tenth year of age, and the children reached adulthood with the thirteenth year. Thirteen years as the date of majority is well documented in Tibetan culture, thus the kings of the Yar-lung dynasty, who established the Tibetan empire during the seventh to ninth century A.D., were enthroned at thirteen (Shakabpa 1967, 27; Stein 1972, 99), though the Dalai Lama, who was king of Tibet since the seventeenth century, was first endowed with full power at the age of eighteen. When the youth attained his majority, no rites, or ceremonial handing-over of any insignia and no admission to any secret fraternity took place, and therefore maturing was merely an assimilating process in former Tibet. Shades of differences in the status of a sixteen year old, unmarried boy and that of a married one of eighteen years remained rather undiscernible. Age and a deeper experience of life were the only prerequisites for being considered an adult.

The youth always socialized with members of the opposite sex; they were co-educated in small private schools and at home they also were never segregated. As the Tibetan youth spent most of his time working in the fields and pastures of his family, certain parts of his engagement showed a distinct romantic flair. To tend the far-off herds of yaks, *'bri*, sheep, and goats or to gather wood and manure for fuel offered him ample opportunity to meet girls, and vice-versa, to tease each other, and to express one's feeling in riddles and songs. The youths, both girls and boys, also met each other at the rare secular feasts, when they all enjoyed themselves with *chang* drinking, dancing and singing. The dancer formed up in two lines, one for each sex, and stepped forwards and backwards in alternation. The song melodies followed given patterns though the text was invented spontaneously; they were sung in alternation, first by the choirs of girls and women and then by the boys and men. Several kinds of drinking songs existed, and my informants laughed when they told about them. Obviously, the content was not as sober and decent as it should have been if to be revealed to a foreigner. Naturally, young people enjoyed the dancing and singing more than the elderly, but otherwise there was no distinction between youths and adults in participating in the festivals. A single visible difference existed between married and unmarried women, i.e. the unmarried girls did not wear the "gay apron", however this custom is slowly dying out today.

Unlike many other traditional cultures, the Tibetan one offered unmarried people the possibility of remaining single. Members of this social group were of marriageable age and did not belong to the clergy; though they were not married, they could have sexual relations with persons of the opposite sex. Sometimes they would live like a couple in a single household. These bachelors recruited new members from families where the elder brother or sister was married and had taken over the parents' farm. If the brother did not invite them to join in a common household or a polyandrous marriage, the younger brothers had to leave, although this was rather seldom, because most young men preferred a quasi-fraternal marriage. Within our hundred-county there were several spinsters. When their elder brothers had married and established families in houses of their parents, a small new house was constructed beneath to shelter the sister now living as a spinster. Further, she received her share of the family's herds, clothes, food-stores, and - provided the family was wealthy - horses, yaks and gold. The bachelor or spinster held his own fortune and set up a small though independent economic unit, though due to the lack of enough manpower he was thrown back upon his brothers' and sisters' help. This help was always given by the relatives, which implied for the bachelor the duty to help at their farm, if necessary.

If in the course of time the spinster got married, every effort was made to prevent the family from splitting up. The younger sister's husband was then usually employed as a caravaneer, herdsman, and so on, on the farm of his brother-in-law. If he was loyal to his wife's family, the segregation was insignificant and his own limited economic abilities were supplemented by his wife's family. If, however, it was a younger bachelor brother who intended to marry, he, too, was incorporated in the working process on his elder brother's farm, in order to prevent him from moving to his wife's family as a *mag pa*.

Old People:

In Tibet the status of old people was not as distinguished as it was in traditional China, though the normative system of Tibetan society demanded reverence and respect for the elderly, above all one's own parents. Everyone was meant to address them with friendliness and kindness and keep the best of food, clothing, or anything else for them. But these standards were only partly kept in real Tibetan society. Commonly the elders' pecularities were tolerated, just as those of the children were; for instance, everyone was inclined to agree verbally with the old persons' claims, but nobody expected these words would ever be put into action. The cohabitation of young and old was then harmonious when the elders kept to their own role, i.e. devoting their life totally to religion and abstaining from interference with the decision making process in family affairs or exercising authority over their families and farms. When these limitations were overstepped, the harmony of the family suffered a severe blow and the son's family usually left the common household, which meant that the extended family of several generations broke into two or more nuclear families.

The adult son could usually expect his father to hand over the farm to him in the course of time. Some informants told me the story of a family where the old father, who was said to have been over eighty, kept all responsibility to himself and treated his son like a child. Everyone in the village was amused and wondered how this family managed.

The old peoples' tasks were reduced as their physical abilities became more and more limited. Society assumed that a man of advanced age would just turn his prayer wheel and utter *oṃ maṇi padme hūṃ* "for the welfare of all sentient beings", as Buddhist scriptures prescribe. This was highly esteemed in popular opinion, and an old man or woman without any relatives or off-spring was therefore cared for by his or her landlord, who provided him with food, clothing and a shelter without any return of labour. But these cases were very rare, because a childless couple would usually adopt an alien child and educate and train him so that he might look after his adoptive parents when they became old and disabled; as a reward he inherited the farm after their deaths.

The care of grandparents and parents was principally the responsibility of the children. Which of the children actually cared for their parents depended upon individual circumstances. Sometimes the parents stayed for a certain period with each of their children; this was to prevent the children from being bothered by them too much, and to prevent their parents also, from suffering too much from a single child's ill temper.

The mere fact of being old was not automatically prestigious, nor did it give any reason for contempt. If in ancient Tibet, during the reign of the Yar-lung kings, old people were not treated respect-

Plate 2. Old woman in her traditional dress and ornaments, typical of the Gyantse area.

fully, this attitude has long since vanished (Stein 1972, 99). I was unable to trace any survival of this custom. Old parents and indeed every old man and woman were especially appreciated if they possessed qualities and abilities of some repute.

Marriage and Divorce

The same formalities were undertaken if one was choosing a bride or groom for one's son or daughter. During the period under investigation the ways of finding a suitable mate changed seriously. I was given much seemingly contradictory information by the former inhabitants of this county; the differences turned out to be related to the informant's age. I shall first describe the traditional system of choosing a mate.

The parents of a boy who was ready to be married came to an understanding as to who would be the best spouse for their son and then addressed themselves to the parents of their choice (Bell 1928, 175). Both lots of parents managed to direct their children's interest towards each other; the boy and girl were asked to collect together some wood or manure for fuel, or they tended the cattle together. If they did not exhibit a sheer disgust for each other, they would certainly become married. Before the marriage, an astrologer was asked whether any serious obstacle was apparent and if the candidates would be able to live together in harmony. Sometimes the parents chose several girls from which one would definitely become their son's wife. If neither the parents nor the son liked a particular girl, the names of all candidates were written on small pieces of paper, which were then shaped with clay in tiny pills of similar size. The parents visited a temple and asked an oracle priest to put the pills into a bowl, which he twisted until the first pill jumped out. The name on the slip of paper indicated the final candidate. If the son rejected the girl allotted to him by the oracle as being the wrong choice, the parents had to start again from the beginning. All candidates whose names had originally been submitted to the oracle were dropped and the parents looked for other girls suitable for their son.

When the final candidate was selected, either by the parent's or the oracles's decision or by the boy's favour, the father visited the girl's parents and presented them with a white scarf (*kha btags*) and a mug of beer, called *slong chang*, which means "asking beer". At this point he started the formal discussion of betrothal. This process was repeated three times and the engagement was thus settled.

Because of the fear of incest, Tibetan custom required that a son would reveal his wishes and preferences for a future wife only to his father and a daughter to her mother. Most of the informants assured me that many of the young people felt ashamed to indicate any favour for a member of the opposite sex; in these cases the parents themselves chose a suitable girl for their son. The same process was applied if parents wished their daughter to be engaged and married with a *mag pa*, a man who will stay with his wife's family. The custom of parental choice of a spouse was much in use among the governmental tax-payers even during the last decades of old Tibet.

In later times, i.e. starting with the period after the XIIIth Dalai Lama's departure, the marriage system changed as the wishes of the young boy or girl became more important.[14] This change primarily affected the lower and lower middle classes. For instance, the hired worker emphasized that individual preference was the single factor for choosing a mate, and that besides regulations preventing incestuous marriages, no other restrictive measures were legitimate.

But this is not the end of the story since the landlords, of both man and woman, had to grant their permission unless the couple belonged to the same landlord though, even then, he had to be informed of their intentions before a marriage could be planned. Nevertheless, the economic situation and the taxes to be paid by each family out of which the young couple might marry had a serious impact on marriage negotiations; and, last but not least, one of the landlords had to agree to accept a small *mi bogs* for losing a worker. The feeling was imparted that a considerable number of herdsmen and hired workers preferred to live in a common-law association. They themselves were never concerned about the legal or illegal status of their marriage, they simply lived with a wife and thought themselves to be married, though on a more official level this was not conclusive. The scholar inquiring into the Tibetan marriage system might be misled because people living in illegal marriage-like communities would confess that neither the landlord nor anybody else could interfere with love affairs or marriage negotiations.

Middle class tenants of the private estates kept apart from both extremes. They gave more importance to the young people's preference than the governmental tax-payers did, while the parents still proceeded to arrange the marriage.

The choice of a mate was based on certain criteria. All informants gave preference to qualities which harmonized well with the society norms. Most desirable was an honest and truthful character, who got on well with the community, and avoided any quarrels; diligence and industry were also appreciated. Wealthy middle-class families also emphasized the prosperity of the future husband's or wife's family. Large property or wealth were not much sought after due to the conviction that a big gap in economic background might lead to disharmony in the young married couple. Theoretically a marriage between the children of a landlord and a tenant might happen, though reality proved it to be rare, and the few known examples were viewed as exceptional. Love and individual preference were discounted as reasons for choosing a mate, and were mentioned only by some shepherds.

None of the former inhabitants of our investigated area mentioned that they first considered the economic condition and the taxes imposed on a family before starting to discuss whether or not their son or daughter might be a suitable future husband or wife for their own children. Apparently it was beyond their imagination to think of a person not being primarily concerned about the duties of both dependents and how a compromise could be arranged. While discussing their economic conditions, they substantiated my assumption that only those girls and boys were considered as possible mates whose families were in an economic situation similar to their own. Methods of harmonizing the allegiances of both families were described in the chapter on dependence.

Only a few wedding presents of goods and money were given. The bride's mother received "milk money" (*nu rin*) as a reward for having brought up the daughter and bride to be. This "milk-money" consisted of two or three tea-bricks, some butter and money. The actual amount of these gifts depended on the financial situation of the family. For a wealthy family it was common to spend three or four hundred *srang* and a considerable amount of butter, but a normal family might not exceed one or two hundred *srang* and a small amount of butter. Nobody wanted to get into debt by arranging a lavish marriage festival. The man or woman, who would take up residence in his or her mate's house, received his or her share of the family goods, such as clothes, two or three hundred *srang*, sheep and goats depending on the family's property. These goods, brought into the newly established household, remained in the possession of the former owner, who was the only person allowed to determine the use made of them.

The process of marriage consummation has already been described elsewhere, and as our informants agreed on most details, it not necessary to repeat it here.[15]

Most marriages were arranged when the partners were between sixteen and twenty years of age, though it was not unusual for a youth of twenty or more to be still unmarried. Many partners remained only a few years with their first wife or husband. This seemed partly due to the high death rate of women, and also to the frequency of divorce (Bell 1928, 194; Carrasco 1959, 47; Aziz 1978, 180ff). A divorced partner was not discriminated against; even if a woman left her husband, she suffered no loss in her reputation. If a man's wife died, he preferred to marry her sister or another relative of hers. After divorce the second marriage was preferably based on love, which means that a sexual relationship with the second wife had already been established while the husband was still married to his first wife. If a man wished to remarry, no one, neither parents nor relatives, interfered: thus the second marriage showed all the characteristics of a love-marriage.

The flight from Tibet and a new life abroad gave stability to Tibetan families. 80% of the informants still lived with their first wife, when interviewed by me, though they claimed that about 40% of their parents had re-married. Several reasons may explain this development: The social isolation which affected most Tibetans in exile induced them to cling still closer to the few persons who had shared their former life. The wife or husband is viewed as part of one's native country. Furthermore, the social environment of the place of exile exerts a hidden force on the Tibetans, who are frequently over-concerned to assimilate the standards of their hosts. In Western countries the Tibetan who wants to be divorced from his or her partner has to face an intricate bureaucracy, which, to him, seems almost impenetrable. All these reasons hamper his inclination for getting divorced.

In Old Tibet the sons stayed with their father and the daughters with their mother, when the parents separated from each other. This was a common rule, though other regulations may have existed if, for instance, a son did not wish to live with his father, or a mother seemed unable to take care of her daughters. The wife took her former possessions with her, if she lived in her husband's home. But if she had offended her husband publicly, she had to compensate him with a suitable amount of goods or money. The same regulation was valid, if the husband had mistreated or beaten his wife. The actual amount of this reward depended on the strength and power of the offended person's family. If the marriage was divorced on mutual agreement, all property except the land was equally divided between husband and wife.

Functions of the Family

Each partial entity of a large super-ordinate system had some function for the totality of this system (Johnson 1960, 56f). The family takes on some of the functions to make society run more smoothly. In old Tibet the essential functions of the family were to act as a productive unit, to provide economic security, to attribute a certain status, to satisfy emotions, to give birth to and educate the offspring. Family life as such was in Tibet less pronounced than in other traditional cultures (Aziz 1969, 160f). This is often claimed to have been due to the predominance of monkhood and its ideals, which idealised the renouncement of one's family, as well as to the affluent local mobility of a considerable part of the total population, that was constantly wandering about either on pilgrimages or business. It may be added that Tibetans preferred to live together in small primary groups which fulfilled many of the tasks of a family. Among the members of such a primary group, the feeling of being a stranger, an outsider, or of not belonging to the others, was virtually non-existent.

As long as the pattern of behaviour was not interfered with it was meaningless whether the babies were looked after by their own mothers, aunts, grand-mothers, or by a neighbour's wife. Some children obviously had a child/mother relationship with all female members of their primary group. Though we must not overlook several stories in Tibetan history which tell of the harsh fate of orphans or semi-orphans; the Tibetan poet-saint Mi-la-ras-pa was one of these poor children. I was also told by Tibetan refugees that semi-orphans often suffered merciless treatment from their relatives. Family weakness was also apparent in the frequent adoptions and transfers to another family.

The main function of a Tibetan family was to set up an economic unit of production, and taxes and services were imposed on the family as a whole as long as it stayed on its farm. As already discussed only the farmer-families of the monastery estate were different. As a common rule the actual amount of these assessments was not based upon the number or age of the family members; on the contrary, these obligations remained stable and were imposed on all who lived on a particular farm. If there were not enough adults in the family to manage the farm, a stranger was often adopted to make up for the lack of workers. As far as duties and rights are concerned these adopted members were just about equal to members of the family by birth. The number of these units of production as well as the number of families remained stable for long periods, as the division or merging of farms was usually not allowed. The system of fraternal polyandry also helped to keep the number of families stable.

Several functions which traditionally are fulfilled by the family were executed by the primary group in Tibet, as for instance the soothing of emotions, the training of children, as well as, at least to some extent, the biological reproduction and education of the children. But nevertheless, the family was never replaced as a productive unit by any other institution, while all other functions of a family might be taken over, though insufficiently, by primary groups. For this reason arranging a marriage concerned the whole primary group and had to be approved by it, while the individual, emotional qualities were neglected.

The individual's economic security was intertwined with the family's acting as a unit of economic production. No one had to face individual poverty or suffer want as long as he stayed within the community of his extended family, though he was limited in his rights as individual proprietor and did not enjoy the full scope of disposing his goods and wealth at will. As a rule, to lose one's family was synonymous with losing one's security, and that pushed the individual into an existential crisis. The feeling of anxiety, of being endangered, typical of so many Tibetans in exile, is based on this bitter experience. The family was responsible for providing economic security for each member, even if he or she had temporally left the family as in the case of a family member joining a monastery. The family had to support, at least partially, even the son in a far away monastery. His share of the family property was managed by a trustee, who delivered the profit to the far-off proprietor.

As each family held a certain position within the social stratification, all its members derived their individual status predominantly from that of the family. A baby held the same status as the family in to which it was born, and in traditional societies the individual was incapable of changing this inherited status. A good example of this system is provided by the Indian caste-system. Tibetan society however, was not as strict as the latter, but usually one's descent from a certain family gave one a certain status and image, and opened or closed certain careers to one. Among the rural population in Tibet this system became institutionalized, as the son inherited his father's status, property, and duties for taxes and service, so did the daughter inherit her mother's. The assignment of status happened within unilineal relationships, though kinship was understood as being bilateral, that means, that the relatives of both parents formed the totality of one's kinship;[16] seemingly, two different social kinship systems were superimposed on each other. This inherited status could be changed only to a limited extent, as opportunities for upward social mobility were very scarce. Among some Tibetan societies prevailing in the East of Khams and Amdo, along with status, the duty of executing a blood-feud was inherited, though in the investigated area of our hundred-county things like that never happened.

Emotional needs such as the longing for warmth, a mutally trusting atmosphere, and a basic appreciation of one's own personality were satisfied within the family, though in traditional Tibet contact with members of the primary group was so intimate that these emotional longings were therein partially fulfilled. This may be indicated by the numerous skin-to-skin contacts habitual among the members of a primary group.[17] Greeting high ranking clerics, noblemen used to bow down and touch foreheads. Similar gestures were common among adults and children: each pressed his forehead against the other's. Among young people erotic teasing was always connected with tactile contact and ranged from simply touching the other's hand or body to imitating sexual intercourse.

Sexual activity was not limited to married couples, as sexual relations existed before and during the marriage. This was valid for men as well as for women. Housing conditions promoted the absence of sexual restrictions, as many households had only a single sleeping-room for all family members, i.e. the kitchen; the nomads' tents without any compartments also facilitated any contact. Also in the inns throughout the country one could meet under the cover of darkness without remembering anything in the morning. Subsequently children were born whose father was not the husband of the mother. If the woman showed discretion and avoided offending the cheated husband, nobody cared if the child was born from an extra-marital relationship. Thus, the sexual drive was primarily satisfied within the family, i.e. between husband and wife, though a considerable flexibility allowed for several other sexual relationships. On average the Tibetan marriage offered both husband and wife a fair opportunity for realizing their innate longings channelizing their sexuality, though love and sex were not strictly limited to the legal marriage. The more educated people read love romances translated from the original Sanskrit into Tibetan and thus the Indian norms and standards concerning love also played a certain, though limited, role in Tibetan life.

The biological reproduction of any society is indissolubly connected with sexual rules. As a rule Tibetan children were legitimate, though a considerable number were begotten by pre- or extra-marital relations. Furthermore, single women usually also gave birth to children; though they were never married and despite their many lovers, they experienced no social discrimination, they just had to work harder as they lacked manpower to sustain themselves. To have no children was viewed as an unfavourable omen. Due to the high death-rate of babies and due to the already discussed family-system Tibet did not suffer from any over population as so many Asian countries did, and was able to maintain a population subtly balanced with the natural resources and agricultural opportunities.

One of the major functions of the family is to bring up and to socialize the children, to educate them according to the innate and often unconscious norms and standards of society. In Tibet this function was primarily fulfilled by the family, either nuclear or extended, though the whole primary group assisted in completing this task. The German anthropologist Ludwar has recently published (1975) a study on Tibetan children's socialization as researched in a Nepalese settlement of Tibetan refugees. As her study focussed on present socialization in the milieu of exile in contrast to this one, the results of my inquiries differ from hers to some extent, though the basic conception of education and socialization remains the same. For a full analysis of this topic I refer to that study, as only the main essentials will be elaborated here.

According to my informants, giving birth to a child was seen as a family event, not concerning anyone outside the family. During the pregnancy, an oracle priest was asked if any obstacle endangered the life of the unborn, and the suitable ceremonies were executed. During the birth itself the husband and father kept on with his usual tasks. An elderly woman, usually a relative or the mother of the young woman, assisted her in delivering the child, which occurred from a kneeling position. Immediately after the birth the child and the mother were washed and dressed, and then the father was called to come. Childbirth happened almost in a state of secrecy; no one except the concerned persons were informed of what was happening. No special rites of purification were executed, nor any other ceremonies making the newly born baby a member of society. When the mother had recovered from childbirth, an intimate family-dinner was arranged. During these days the father went to the monastery to ask a Lama for a name to be given to the baby. Only if a previous child had died, a Lama was called to execute ceremonies preventing the dead child from "summoning" the newly born, otherwise the naming was free from any religious rites.

The baby was suckled by the mother beyond the birth of the next child, so for some time the mother had to nurse two children simultaneously. In this way rivalries between sisters or brothers, which often occur when babies are weaned too early (Leighton/Kluckhohn 1972, 147ff), were kept to an absolute minimum. Frequently I watched children of three or four years nestling into their mother's blouse to be fed.[18] A special baby-food did not exist, not even plain milk of cows, *'bri*, or sheep; to promote the children's growth they were fed with Tsampa (*rtsam pa*), parched barley flour mixed with tea, clarified butter, and sugar. The babies were bathed regularly and rubbed with oil and butter. Instead of diapers, fresh wool from lambs or sheep were stuffed into a small leather bag, the baby's nest. Infantile death rate was approximately 20 or 30%, though the exact figures were not available due to the vagueness of my informants.

The education of children happened at two stages.[19] The first one started from birth and lasted till the child was about four years old when the second period began and lasted up to the tenth or thirteenth year. During the first period the baby was treated as an irresponsible being whose physical weakness asked for every support and care. At the start of the second phase the child was educated and trained in some easy task. At this second phase the child was confronted with the basics of Buddhist morality, such as "you must not lie, steal, kill, or make any creature suffer!"

When still in the first phase the baby was cared for with utmost love and tender affection. Whenever the baby started to cry the mother gave her breast to soothe the child. The baby's day was not regulated by certain periods, whenever it felt hungry or ready to sleep, everyone did his best to satisfy him. As soon as the child was able to sit up, he was fed by each family member; the tastiest bits were put into his mouth, frequently with the mother's lips. At this point the child never experienced any harsh word and was never spanked; everyone apparently was fond of him, even if he smashed chinaware on the floor or beat up his brothers and sisters.

Everyone living in the same household and even neighbours established a very intimate skin-to-skin relationship with the little child. Adults pressed their foreheads against the child's as already mentioned above. The child was hugged all day long; he shared his mother's bed till a new baby was born and then he moved to his father's bed, thus always wrapped in the warmth of the other's affection. For instance, if the child was caught biting his finger-nail the mother rushed to give him her breast because it was said that the child suffered from lack of affection.

As the Tibetans were very reluctant to reveal anything about their sexual lives, I could only observe some typical behaviour in the field of child sexuality. As a rule, Tibetans view sexuality as a given fact of life in which an adult as well as a child participates. When the child was still very young and naked, it was common to touch the child's genitals and to joke "What's that?" In a Tibetan settlement I watched some women shouting to some boys of about eight years that they should "make love with those girls"; the girls were playing beneath and were about three or four years old. This kind of joking was apparently much in use in Old Tibet.

To summarize the educational implications of this first phase, one might refer to the constantly repeated exhortation "be a sweet [child]!" (*byams po byed*); during the second period of education the children were then admonished to "behave modestly, be industrious!". At this point the child had to learn how to help his family in managing the farm. When he now committed some faults he was severely punished, often physically.

The child had, within this second period, to accept the precepts of Buddhist morality. Almost every informant told me a story of how he was badly beaten by his mother or father, as he was about to kill flies, worms, fish, etc., for fun. Once they had been punished they avoided killing any sentient being for the rest of their lives. Whereas during the first period all the aggresive actions of a small child were answered by jokes and laughter, during the second period the child had to learn how to temper his feelings. Children from wealthy families started at that date to learn how to read and write, and learning Buddhist prayers by heart.

The task of educating children was shared by father and mother, and no basic difference between boys or girls could be observed. From the tenth year onward, lessons in the proper use of agricultural implements were more important than anything else. Some children started at that tender age to leave their parents' home in order to hire themselves out as shepherds or something similar.

The main educational tools used by parents, teachers, and Lamas were verbal commands (*bslabs bya*).[20] These commands reflected the common ideas founded on the Tibetan tradition of Buddhism and passed down for countless generations. These ideas and socially relevant norms set up the structture of a man's behaviour, and in old Tibet, nobody doubted whether or not it might be good to conform to them. A conformative way of life was viewed as a sure way of being sheltered from the dangers of life and having a feeling of security; it further assured a good reputation among one's primary group and the whole of society; it was based on religious ideas and guaranteed a lucky rebirth. Tibetan society offered some freedom to the individual if he complied with the ruling norms and customs of his class. This conviction shaped the way children were educated, as already mentioned. Ideally conflicts between different groups and opposing interests were never precisely formulated but softened by hiding the real issue amidst a lot of soothing words. Thus, Tibetan letters, written in a traditional style, never communicate their meaning in clear statements, but hide it in pure verbiage. This was the common way to treat any problem, and Tibetans were used to searching for the hidden meaning between the lines of displayed friendliness. Tibetans are still convinced that uttering one's own thoughts clearly sometimes insults a person because of contradictory interests and this was viewed as undesirable behaviour due to their religious ideas. Thus, Tibetans tried to phrase their opinions as amicably as possible, but without giving up their original intentions. The ideal of education was to form a personality harmonizing with the group, but never sacrificing one's own individuality.

Throughout the world, going to school is an important part of childhood, but, in regard to our investigation, we have to dwell on school only as it is involved in the education system as a whole, and not as an institution (Richardson 1962, 13f). A public and general school did not exist in Old Tibet. Two different institutions performed the functions commonly carried out by school: the private teachers and the monastic schools. Both institutions taught the children how to read and write, conveyed to them the ideals of society, and provided them with a survey of religion and literature. The administrative academy at Lha-sa was a secondary school and for this reason falls outside the scope of this investigation (Brauen 1974, 137f). The monastic school made no serious impact on the social and educational system of the area, as only a small number of boys joined the monastery and were educated there. Thus, only the private teacher remains to be discussed.

Most commonly the pupils went to the teacher's home for their lessons. Those boys whose home was too far away to go to and fro every day stayed with their teacher and joined his household, while the parents supported them financially. In many cases the teacher was a friend or relative of the boys' parents which prompted the original idea to have the children educated by him. The teacher did not have to have any exam or diploma; if he had something to teach, it was thought to be sufficient. No fees were charged to the pupil's parents for attending the classes, though the parents were commonly expected to offer some goods and agricultural products to the teacher; these offerings and donations were strictly related to the family's economic situation. This was an institutionalized custom and nobody thought of avoiding it, primarily because the teacher had to sustain himself by these gifts. The steward of the noble estate had attended a private teacher's classes for six years, and this period was thought enough to make him an educated and reputable man.

The noble landlord had established a school at the district capital for his own as well as his tenants' and subjects' children. In this case the teacher was chosen and paid by the landlord himself. Every child of the landlord's subjects had free access to this school, although the family had to bear the loss of a young working child. It was because of this that only wealthy tenants and farmers managed to send their children to school at the district capital. The establishment and maintenance of this school was a highly renowned fact among all the noble's subjects, though this was not as unique as one might guess, as we learn from Bell (1928, 104, 201) and Richardson (1962, 13f). A lively story of a child attending such a school is related by Taring (1970, 29ff), a lady of the Tibetan nobility. Despite this schooling opportunity the majority of country people as well as almost all women were illiterate. Only a few girls picked up some reading ability by casually listening when their brothers memorized the texts.

Adoption and Change of Family

Adoption was the single solution to the threatened extinction of a family where no suitable offspring had been produced capable of taking over the farm and the duties levied by the landlord. This situation occured for instance, when the only son fervently desired to join a monastery, or when no son was born to the parents, or when he turned out to be incapable of managing a farm, and when their daughter did not marry a *mag pa*, a man joining the family. Adoption was also practised if a dispute disunited a family. As an enlargement of family and farm-units was outside the scope of the Tibetan social system, the seceding member had to look for another family willing to adopt him. Such a case happened in the village of the governmental tax-payers and was reported to me by the person concerned, as follows:

The person in concern, whom we shall call Ego,[21] was born the eldest son of family A, who belonged to the government tax-payers. After his birth his mother left family A by divorce. When his father remarried, he favoured the son of his second marriage. Despite the custom of passing down the farm to the eldest son, the father designated the son of his second marriage, Ego's stepbrother, to inherit the farm and all properties (*pha ghzi*). When the sibling married a daughter of one of the government tax-payer families a serious quarrel arose between Ego and the sibling, who was supported by their father, and Ego had to leave his family. Despite this, his family, which we called A, provided him with a small house and some fields. The community of all governmental tax-payers (*khral pa'i spyi ba*) decided that this particular plot would be re-united with the property of family A, when Ego joined another governmental tax-payer family; that is if such a family agreed to adopt him. A little later the council of governmental tax-payers declared that Ego should now belong to family D, which was also a governmental tax-payer family with a single daughter. She was married to a man of another subject-category, and the couple lived on the farm of the wife's parents (matrilocal marriage). Soon a quarrel arose between Ego and his adoptive family (called D). When the council of government tax-payers once more discussed the problem, they resolved that family D had to be divided into a main family and a branch, called family D1. (In Tibetan to the actual family name, for instance *nag-pa*, was added the syllable *zur*, that means *nag-zur*). The total property as well as the duties and taxes levied from family D were then shared between the two branches.

VI. GROUPS AND NORMS

The Primary and Secondary Group

In the preceding chapters I have often referred to the primary groups and their central role in assisting the family in exercising its social funtions. Before going into details we shall discuss what is implied by the term "primary group". The Austrian sociologist Wössner (1971, 102, 106) states that primary groups are to be qualified by various marks: 1. The various members of a primary group share a common living place; they know each other very well by sight. 2. Each individual member is fully integrated into the group, which provides a strong "we-feeling". 3. The relationships among the individual members are not fully defined to a single role or function, thus they are called "diffuse". Most relationships are based on emotion and particularly addressed to a certain person; if one of its members leaves the whole group is affected.

If this concept is applied to Tibetan society, we recognize that several primary groups like circles centring around the Ego showed a diminution of their characteristics the further they got from the centre, i.e. the Ego. The first and most intimate primary group was formed by the family to which also the servants belong; in Tibetan they were called *nang mi*, that means "men of the interior", i.e. of the household. The second primary group consisting of the neighbourhood group (*grong pa khyim tshe*) resembles the first very much. Within this study it is simply called a "primary group". The next grade consisted of the friends and trustees of a person; in Tibetan these people were called *dga' sa yag sa*, which means "a good place is a place of joy". This is a more colourful expression and was synonymous with *dga' po nye bo*, "a pleasant friend". The next group centred around one's landlord, while the most extensive primary group was set up by the inhabitants of a county or a certain valley. These people were called *pha yul gcig pa*, "those who have the same fatherland".

Western life shows many groups that are set up through the initiative and desire of their members, as for instance a sports or country club, and they make up a unique characteristic of our modern life. In traditional Tibet the voluntary groups were rather insignificant; within our "hundred county" only two such groups existed, which were established by the free will of their members.

Among the governmental tax-payers, there prevailed a religious brotherhood, called the "Manibrotherhood". Its main function was, in theory, to utter the Mantra of Avalokitesvara, i.e. *oṃ maṇi padme hūṃ*; the members in practice met together in order to share a friendly drink. This group has already been discussed when dealing with the characteristics of the governmental tax-payers as a social class. Similar brotherhoods occurred in other parts of Old Tibet, and were frequently addressed as *skyid sdug tshogs pa*, "groups [to share] joy and sorrow". Today such groups may be observed among Tibetans in exile.

The second group consisted of men who joined together in order to hunt. As the Tibetan government had banned the unnecessary killing of animals, due to the Buddhist ethics, these men had to work secretly. As none of my informants admitted to having participated in these hunting activities, they were unable to contribute any details. The village headman obviously knew some of the hunters, but he claimed to know nothing about hunting magic and sorcery. The bond which united this group was the secret hunting, so it played no significant role within the social life of the village.

The craftsmen were commonly enrolled in guilds, but on village level there were no specific craftmen's groups. Thus, if only a single carpenter, and a single silver-smith lived in a certain village, each belonged to his individual guild. Nor was the social life among the members of a certain guild stimulating; once a year all members gathered at the district capital to select those who had to work for the government as a part of their assessments during the year. Other than this yearly meeting the members had no contacts.

The blacksmiths were organized in associations, too. Seemingly these organizations granted their members a certain security and a strong feeling of solidarity (Rauber-Schweizer 1976, 69ff). The blacksmiths were one of the few groups in traditional Tibet that exercised endogamy, that means that they married only among their own group. As this craft belonged to the ill-reputed professions, nobody was inclined to communicate full details about the blacksmiths. For a more elaborate discussion I refer the reader to Rauber-Schweizer (op.cit.). Among the informants interviewed by me no blacksmith was available, and only a silver-smith related his life story to me.

The Pattern of Social Norms

To analyse the social system of a civilization without referring to the norms which give origin to its distinct behaviour and preferences, so important for any social life, would mean to describe only the issues and never to seek for the motivations. Certainly, the norms of any civilization make a far more subtle pattern than its social structures.

As to Tibetan society, hitherto nobody has dared to write a chapter or a paper on the norms that mould the Tibetan way of life. I, too, feel inadequate for this task and I shall just suggest some ideas for setting up a pattern of norms, well aware of the incompleteness and one-sidedness of the attempt.

H. Richardson (1962, 11) says that in the past as well as present times, one of the Tibetans' national characteristics was that everyone's ideas and actions were strongly influenced by their devotion to religion. Therefore, we shall first discuss the impact on the social system exercised by religion. Till 1959 Tibet remained a country explicitly oriented towards her own Buddhist tradition. When Buddhism spread to Tibet from the 7th century on, the Tibetan kings emphasized the new religion as the uniquely valid ethical basis for the whole people. Though at the actual time when the kings started to propagate Buddhism this remained an ideal far from reality, still, after a single century, Buddhism exerted an ever increasing influence on all levels of every-day life. This is well documented by a manuscript unearthed at the Tun-huang caves (H.E. Richardson 1977, 221). The dominance of Buddhism in Tibet was never touched by any of the main currents of world history shattering so many civilizations. The muslims never conquered central Tibet, neither did Genghiz Khan's army, nor the colonial powers of the West.

The religious man, not only the celibate monk, became a person of high repute, who set up new standards for everybody. Indian civilization reached Tibet together with the Buddhist doctrine (7th to 12th centuries AD); every kind of science and human art was intertwined with Buddhist conceptions. Thus, the Tibetans failed to create a secular scholarly philosophy. Be it medicine, astronomy or poetry - every discipline of the human mind was involved in religion. On this issue the monasteries became the only places for higher education and every talented young Tibetan had to become a member of a monastery to receive scholarly training and to be able to exercise his gifts later on.

In this way the country people envisaged the clergy not just as religious people, but also as the only educated ones; everybody who was able to read and write originated from the clergy and contributed to the normative force of this class. Thus, country people accepted, at least verbally, all the norms set up by religion and its supporters.

These religiously based norms were taught to the people by the religious teachers and Lamas, who coined their thoughts and moral advices into the "exhortations" (*bslabs bya*), already mentioned above. Throughout these exhortations three virtues out of the six *pāramitā* were recommended; alms giving, moral conduct, and patience. All informants agreed that these virtues - together with diligence

Plate 3. Tibetan farmers at tea-break.

and exertion - made up the ideal man, from a Tibetan point of view.

Some Tibetans failed in complying with this idealistic concept of man's behaviour. The nobles and kings were sometimes ill-reputed for their brutality. As in these two examples: bKra-shis-rnam-rgyal, king of Ladakh during the 16th century, blinded his brother and banished him to a remote village (L. Petech 1977, 28); the tyrant of Nyag-rong was said to have thrown children from the top of his palace and see them burst asunder (R. Kaschewsky/P. Tsering 1973, 459). But we have always to remember that such acts were exceptional.

Hitherto the piety of the Tibetan laity has not been well known, but devoting certain days to religious practice was apparently an important aspect of a layman's spiritual life, and a considerable part of Tibetans participated in these days of meditation. These days were called in Tibetan *bsnyen gnas, bsnyung gnas,* or *smyung gnas*, all referring to Skr. *uposadha*,[1] which means on the eighth, fifteenth, and thirtieth day of the Tibetan lunar month religiously engaged laymen devoted themselves to certain rituals and meditations. On the morning of such a day the laity congregated in the temple and pledged themselves to comply to the vows of the *uposadha*-day. Guided by a locally known Lama, they read together the promise "not to kill any sentient being, even an ant; not to take away anything that belonged to an other person, even if it might be a leaf; to abstain from impure conduct; to abstain from lying; to keep aloof from all intoxicants" as written in a popular ritual text.[2] These vows are the common moral laws for laymen. As a part of the Tibetan people recited this promise monthly, its repetition influenced distinctively their normative thinking. The same applies to the continuous reciting of the Avalokiteśvara-Mantra, i.e. the well known *om mani padma hūm*. All prayers dedicated to Avalokiteśvara, the Great Compassionate, refer to all sentient beings as one's present mother. Thus all living beings became identified with the person closest to one's heart. Due to this concept no being should be killed or tortured, however brutish it might be. The contents of the most recited prayers are useful for exploring the moral norms of Tibetan laity, as by constant repetition these prayers gave rise to distinct normative conceptions and patterns without being understood by reason.[3]

Of course, there are and were a lot of contradictory facts to be met within the Tibetan society, and not every Tibetan was inclined to base his life on religious concepts and ideals. Thus the above rendered image fails to convey the normative thinking outside religion. This is simply due to the lack of information. As are most people, Tibetans too are fond of depicting themselves as pious, law-abiding, and hard-working people. Though only a part of the whole population had really shared this opinion, they would never have told about their diverging inclinations to a foreigner.

A further trait, so characteristic of all traditionally educated Tibetans, is the introversion of the whole society. Tibetans were never fond of anything foreign, they were never interested in their neighbours, least of all in distant countries. If one asks Tibetans about their dreams and wishes, when they were still young children, several will answer that they had thought of becoming a Yogi or a hermit. To explore the real world offered no excitement to the Tibetans. They preferred to introspect their own psyche and to try to disclose the abysses of the human mind. On this inward journey they envisaged the demons and spirits so common to Tibetan thinking and copiously re-presented by Tibetan art.

In the field of Tibetan literature we encounter the biographies and autobiographies of those hermits who exhibited this introversion par excellence. The heroes of the Tibetans were Mi-la-ras-pa, hermit as well as poet, highly gifted mystics like Padmasambhava, who demonstrated the full range of parapsychological abilities, and Ke-sar, the conqueror of all demons. In folk theatre as well as in folk-literature, the historical kings became transformed into saints, exclusively devoted to religion, though historical documents do not agree with this idealistic image.

Some Westerners, such as Sven Hedin and A. David-Neel, who travelled throughout Tibet communicated their experiences as fictitious stories and, typically enough, the heroes of these novels are hermits, mystics or sorcerers, but never emperors or war-lords. Apparently for these authors this was the only way to exhibit their personal feelings about the nature of Tibetan life.

Among the educated classes this introversive tendency might originate from the Buddhist theory of the world's insufficiency and irreality; while among the uneducated commoners the shaman's trance and journey to heaven provided the imagination for being fascinated by one's inner life. This peculiarity of Tibetan character even now seemingly prevents them from desiring to explore the world where they still live. Even such an outrageous event as man's first step on the moon did not give rise to any striving for further knowledge; only a few Tibetan scholars debated it by referring to the cosmography of the *Abhidharmakośa*, a Buddhist philosphic compendium written during the 4th century AD.

The lay morality consisted primarily in abstention from killing and stealing, while emphasizing the opposite, as for instance, freeing animals from being slaughtered or offering alms to monks and beggars. These norms became valid within the investigated county, as hunting and fishing were prohibited as well as showing in public a liking for weapons. Consequently no warriors' dances, or bow-and-arrow contests, etc., occurred there.

Private property was much esteemed and the thief was viewed as an ill-reputed, bad man. The word for thief, *rkun ma*, became an abusive term.

The Tibetans' gift for integrating marginal persons and occurences is unusual. Although within our hundred-county no reliable case was reported to me, I have some examples to back up this statement. In an excellent study M. Goldstein (1964) illustrates this integrative ability with the *ldab ldob*, a kind of overseer and sportsman accepted as an integrated part of the monastic community. If a robber happened to be related to a clergyman — as a high ranking Tibetan intimated to me — the Lama might sometimes say farewell to his robber-brother by wishing him a successful raid. Despite the common disapproval of cannibalism by all Tibetan authorities, at a tiny village in Eastern Tibet a person acting as a body-disposer used to cut off a piece of flesh from the body and roast it at the fire while the funeral ceremonies were performed and the relatives of the dead were still present. His action was neither condemned nor approved by the village people nor by the monks of a near-by monastery who were proud of their high standards in ethics and philosophy. Criminals, especially thieves, were not often caught if they succeeded in escaping beyond the border of their land-lord's principality, because their bad *karma* was viewed as such an unfavourable burden that detecting the criminal seemed to be overacting and unnecessary. This custom of integrating marginal characters apparently hampered minority groups from detaching themselves from the majority. The only duty imposed upon marginal characters was that they had to accept the common usage defining their own realm and the ideological pattern of the whole Tibetan society.

If a thief returned from prison - as reported by the village headman - nobody would offend him openly, though his statements would be accepted with some reserve; commonly his family supplied him with a mule and some victuals enabling him to go to another county. Among the categories of the private subjects criminals had the opportunity of returning to their native village. The treasurer of the estate (*phyag mdzod*) had then to guarantee that the former criminal would not relapse into his previous life. For this reason former criminals were preferably engaged in housework.

Fate, Personality, and Efficiency:

Investigating the social and economic conditions of India it becomes evident that a few religious conceptions do not promote economic efficiency. One might assume that the same statment was valid for Tibetan society, as both — the Hindus in India as well as the Buddhists in Tibet — believed and still believe in *karma*. Karma means that every activity, mental or physical, leaves a virtual trace on the individual's personality. Whenever a future situation will correspond to the quality of such a trace, it will become active and afflict the actual circumstances of one's life. Thus, man shapes his future fate. As a model of this concept one might take of a parallelogram of different divergent powers. As the increase of a single power will affect the whole structure thus each benevolent action will change one's *karma* as a whole.

For this reason Tibetans strive to improve their fate by making offerings to the Buddha and his community. Primarily this is recommended for attaining a favourable rebirth after one's death. Most informants stated that this precisely was the issue of their religious endeavour.

The required offerings consisted in butter for burning in lamps, flour to form sacrificial cakes (*gtor ma*), tea, soup, and more butter for supplying the monks. In order to afford these offerings the basic necessaries had to be satisfied first, and there had to be surplus in production. Thus Tibetan religious tradition required a certain economic efficiency, which was and still is highly appreciated among the whole society. Due to these circumstances the Tibetans seemingly adopted the Western economic system without any serious difficulties. But there is an important and distinct difference between a Tibetan and a Western worker in spending his earnings. The Westerner appreciates money in order to enlarge his standard of living, to consume further goods, while the Tibetan, though he keeps his house decently, spends his savings for religious purposes to secure a favourable rebirth for himself and his family members. Thus the Tibetan is stimulated by his religious tradition to be industrious and efficient.

Certainly, there are as many motivations centred around one's Ego among Tibetan people as there are elsewhere, but it was my intention to demonstrate only some striking facts among the vast range of behaviour and normative thinking.

VII. ECONOMY

General Characteristics

The terrain of the area researched, from deep valleys to 5000 metre high mountains, forced a type of "mixed" economy upon the inhabitants. The land was described by the villagers as being *sa ma 'brog* or *yul ma 'brog* which means "neither farmland nor pastureland"; they practised a mixed 'alpine' agriculture, "Linked with, but not within, the *aBrog pa* are the *Sa Ma aBrog* (neither soil nor high pasturage) – a large segment of pastoralists often labelled 'semi-nomads'. By many criteria – animal husbandry, use of tents, even mobility and the like, - there seems to be no reason for excluding them from the *aBrog pa*, but the Tibetans invariably insist on the distinction." (Ekvall 1968,21)

This definition of the term *sa ma 'brog* is based upon circumstances in Amdo. In the situation researched here, the term *sa ma 'brog* apparently only signifies an alpine-like agriculture; no one in this instance would think of calling the described relationship "semi-nomadic", as the above mentioned distinctive characteristics of such are totally missing.

Both aspect of this type of agriculture, i.e. farming and animal husbandry, are closely related to the use of the soil. Understanding the Tibetan concept of land ownership is essential in an investigation of this sort. Seemingly there was no judicial formulation of rules concerning the possession of land. Only from the customary handling of land could one extract the regulations; these rules were often enforced very differently in different areas of Tibet. The laws concerning landed property described below can be applied at most to only the neighbouring counties. However, the villagers questioned said themselves that there had never been two counties organized under the same system. Even the nearest county had been structured completely differently from their own.

In the particular "hundred-county" researched, land was shared between the three categories of subjects. In principle the government was the highest landlord (Richardson 1962, 15). It could and did reward deserving nobles with land and subjects, as a noble in the service of the state received no salary. The government also granted estates to monasteries, both to maintain the clergy and to meet the costs of lengthy rituals. Land in Tibet was not a commodity to be bought and sold; one could only receive the right to use the soil. This statement was generally valid for all Tibet. The government granted permission for land usage to the upper classes of each category of subjects, governmental tax-payers with large properties and to the monasteries and the nobles, who in turn were obliged to deliver taxes and some manual labour or services to the government. This elite then rented the use of an exactly defined amount of land to settlers. Whenever possession of land is mentioned in this study, then ownership in the special sense of the "right ot use" is meant. In the three villages researched, governmental tax-payers had the right to use the largest area of land. The next largest area was controlled by the noble estate. The monastery only used a small amount of land. Most of the pasturage belonged to the nobility; however, the subjects of the government also had large areas of pasture land; the monastery had only two pastures in use.

The size of an individual field was measured by the amount of seed needed to sow it. This method of measurement is preserved here, because a translation into square metres would include too many uncertain factors. The villagers said that a field was usually large enough to cover the cereal needs of one family. The silversmith reported that he owned two fields, and that each required 20 *khal*, (170 kg) of seed. The yield of the land fluctuated according to the quality of the soil; the best soil produced ten times, the middling quality five times and the poorest land only three times the amount of seed.

A prerequisite for a reasonable crop was proper and expert care of the soil: it was watered, fertilized and rotation of crops was practised. The watering system was simple; water was chanelled from the river and, relying upon the natural fall of the land for power, conducted throughout the fields. The channels were small, open ditches; obstacles were overcome with wooden pipes and the waterflow was regulated by small sluice-boards. The questioned Tibetans decisively denied that any kind of water rights existed, although we know that they were found in other parts of Tibet, for example in Ladakh. They said that each farmer was only responsible for looking after that part of the water system that ran on his land. Arguments probably only very rarely occurred because there was enough water in the area anyway. Mechanical water wheels and other such machines were unknown.

To improve the soil, Tibetans fertilized the land in the winter with animal and human waste. One could also improve the land by sowing "heavy barley" (*sa bon lci ba*), a tall large grained type of barley. On good soil one planted "light barley" (*sa bon yang ba*) which was shorter with smaller grains and had a much higher yield per field than "heavy barley". These two crops were rotated with each other and, after a certain amount of time, the field was left to lie fallow for a year.

Barley was the primary crop, from which the staple food, *rtsam pa*, was produced. Other food grown included potatoes, radishes, cabbage, carrots and onions. Peas grew only in the lower settlement of the noble estate. Fruit did not grow at all. Abundant Chinese mushrooms (*mu-erh*) grew wild in the area, but were not often used as food.

The harvest was carried home on the backs of yaks and donkeys, where it was stored on the roof or in side buildings whose rooms were used for drying foodstuffs. If a farmer had no beasts of burden, then he either had to borrow animals from his neighbours or carry the harvest home on his own back.

Agricultural implements used by Tibetans farmers included ploughs, which were made of wooden shafts (*thong mda'*) capped with iron spikes (*thong lcogs*); shovels and spades (both called *'jag ma*), and hoes that are similar to pick axes with wide blades (*tog 'tse*, called *'jor* in Lha-sa). A wooden beam was used as a harrow and was weighted by the farmer himself who stood with wide-spread legs on the beam and so rode around the field. Tools were made on request by carpenters and smiths who came into the home; sometimes ready-made implements could be bought, but they were never made by the farmers themselves.

In animal husbandry, sheep raising held the most important place and was pursued mainly on the noble estate. Herds of over 3000 head of sheep were not uncommon. Goats were also raised but they were not fed domestically and even in winter were not kept in stalls but stayed in fenced meadows half-way up the mountains. Although the sheep multiplied prolifically, spring brought the threat of a reduction in the number of animals because of the scarcity of food and the low resistance of the weakened ewes and newly born lambs to disease. The keeping of herds was extensive but deliberate breeding to produce better animals was not practised. Swine were not raised; it seems as if pig breeding was due to Chinese influence and therefore was relatively rare in central and western Tibet. Chickens were raised only for their eggs and ducks were unknown.

Large stock included yak and *'bri*,[1] donkeys, mules and horses; *mdzo mo*,[2] a cross between a yak and a cow, were not raised in the researched area. It was said that the climate was not suitable for these animals although sometimes a *mdzo mo* was bought from one of the nearby markets because it gave more milk than a *'bri*. The large herds of yak and *'bri* belonging to the noble estate also remained unsheltered on the mountains the whole winter through and received no fodder. When a farmer owned only a few animals then they stayed in the stall that was the groundfloor of the family house. Even this stock was not fed, but driven to the grazing meadows on the mountains. Generally, there was as little conscious breeding of large stock as of sheep and goats. The yak-tender of the noble family was the only one who knew anything about animal disease and medicine.

Plate 4. Tibetan farmers with a plough that was in use until recent times.

The Economic System of Government Tax-Paying Subjects

Agriculture and Husbandry:

The eight, or originally just seven, families of subjects who paid taxes to the government owned the right to use all fields and meadows that belonged to the social category of governmental subjects. Since large surface area measurements were unknown, the boundary was determined by natural landmarks such as buildings, cliffs, waterfalls, etc. The government had lent the land at some time- the villagers whom we questioned could not even approximate the date - the community of governmental tax-paying subjects (*khral pa spyi pa*). The village-headman called this act of enfeoffment *ches 'gros bzhes thang* which means something like "the command of great importance".

Altogether this land measured from 800 to 1000 *khal* (10800 - 13500 kg) of seed. Each of the eight tax-paying families owned a part of the common land; the individual tracts seemed relatively large, generally needing 100-150 *khal* (1350 - 2425 kg) of seed. Families that had been split up through quarrels owned correspondingly less land. Then there were also the extra large families that owned more than the usual amount of land. The lending of this land and its size was officially documented in the so-called *sa leb rtsis* ("statistical registration of the measure of the land"). The land under the jurisdiction of the governmental tax-payers contained some of the best soil available and so produced some ten times the seed originally sown. The category of governmental subjects hardly ever farmed land of the poorest quality which only yielded three times the seed sown, in contrast to the subjects of the noble land-lord who did have to till the bad land. Even the governmental subjects whose farmland was only half as large as the normal allotment could harvest 400 - 500 *khal* (5400 - 6750 kg) per year to sell at a pure profit. Considering their assets alone, the governmental tax-payers were rightly called large scale farmers.

The possession of animals under the governmental tax-payers was variable. Some families had 1000 - 2000 sheep and goats, 100-200 yak and *'bri* and up to 15 horses; others, like the village headman (*rgan po*), owned only sheep and a few yak to be used as beasts of burden. These animals were often watched over by paid shepherds who were the private employees of rich farmers. The governmental subjects were not familiar with the complicated animal leasing system adopted by the subjects of the noble estate. If a *'bri* was lent under the system "without birth - without death" (*skyes med 'chi med*), the tenant was to deliver 1 *khal* (13.5 kg) of butter to the proprietor per year for each *'bri* leased. The number of animals in the herd stayed the same, at least as far as the butter fee was concerned. Any increase or reduction of the herd was the concern of the shepherd or farmer alone, which meant that every calf born belonged to him and that every animal that died had to be replaced by a new one. This contract could continue through many decades and even centuries. The "three ewes, two lambs" system, relevant to the sheep raising of the noble estates, did not exist under the governmental subjects.

Taxes and Required Services:

The duties and taxes of the whole of the eight tax-paying families (*khral pa spyi pa*) were also recorded in an official document (Goldstein 1971 a, 6). This type of taxation, in which the whole category of governmental subjects in a certain village is given a lump sum of taxes and service to be delivered is called *lung pa'i khral* or "county-tax". The responsibility for punctually delivering the tribute was carried by all of the eight families together. The village headman (*rgan po*) then presented the taxes to the castle of the district governor (*rdzong dpon*). This collective tax was divided according to the various products to which the government laid claim.

The tendency to pay in money had increased in the last decades although the old names for the individual products were kept. This collective levy was understood to be the tribute from the landed properties belonging to all the governmental tax-payers. The individual assessments were:

1. A tax paid in goods (*dngos rigs*): needles, awls, earrings, socks, *rtsam pa*, *chang* (a sort of beer); altogether worth 30 *srang*; later this tax was lowered to 22 *srang*.
2. Cash-tax (*dngul skyang*): 30 *srang*.
3. Meat-tax (*sha khral*): 92 *khal* (1242 kg); this tax was not allowed to be paid in the equivalent amount of money.
4. Grain-tax (*'bru khral*): 128 *khal* (1728 kg) and an additional 10 *khal* (135 kg) for the dGa'-ldan monastery.
5. Tsampa-tax: 15 *khal* (202.5 kg).
6. Hay-tax (*rtsa khral*): 10 *tam ga* or 15 *sho*.
7. Wood-tax (*shing khral*): 300 *rgya ma* (810 kg).
8. Butter-tax (*mar khral*): 46 *khal* (621 kg).

Some of these taxes were not given to the district governor but instead to certain monasteries; the meat tax, for example, was used to feed the monks during the *sMon-lam* festival in Lha-sa and the grain tax was presented to the dGa'-ldan monastery. However, these taxes were not levied by the monasteries themselves but by the State, which designated them to the monasteries as a donation from the government. So as not to complicate the transference of the goods unduly, the tax was given directly to the monastery.

When the tax was to be paid in money instead of actual goods the amount was determined yearly by a committee of the district administration (*rdzong*).

Usually one *khal* of grain was considered equivalent to 20 *sho*, so that the community had to pay 70 *srang* instead of 128 *khal* of grain. This was a relatively good rate of exchange.[3] The collective tax-load carried by the eight governmental tax-payers amounted to ca. 500 *do tshad* per year. Since Tibet had experienced rapid inflation in the years following the thirteenth Dalai Lama, i.e. after 1933, the rate of assessment was higher in its actual value before the period in which the informants lived.

The dividing of the tax burden was an internal affair of the community. A distribution key was used for this purpose. In this key, a duty on possessions as well as a kind of duty on family members was provided for. It was based upon the mathematical figure of a *rkang*; this term was also used by the other two categories of subjects but in a different sense. For the governmental tax-payers, a *rkang* denoted a specific unit of measurement that was used to determine the distribution of the tax load among the governmental families (whereas the categories of noble and monasterial subjects used the term *rkang* to designate a work-group of a specific size that was to work under the landlord in fulfilment of its manual labour duty.) Work teams were not formed from the families of governmental tax-payers because, in contrast to the two other categories, they did not have any compulsory duties to provide beyond the transport service and even that was usually paid for in some other way. One *rkang*, in the sense of the term used by the governmental tax-payers, was divided into six **phu lu*; one **phu-lu* was the smallest unit of measurement in the computation of assessments. Eleven *sho* (i.e. 1 *srang* and 1 *sho*) were to be paid as tax for one **phu lu*. The following integers were all assessed at one **phu lu* of tax each:

1. Family members over 18 and under 75 years of age, regardless of sex.
2. The home.
3. Twenty-two donkeys or cows.
4. 18 yak, *'bri* or horses.
5. 112 sheep and goats.

Each family out of the governmental tax-payers had to pay these taxes to the community of all governmental tax-payers (*khral pa spyi ba*). Money that had already been paid, for instance for pasturage etc., was subtracted from the sum total. This money, collected from the eight tax-paying families, formed, along with other revenue, the basis of the collective tax to be paid yearly. The total tax liability of the eight governmental tax-paying families amounted to 14 *rkang*, i.e. 84 **phu lu* worth 924 *sho*. In order to determine the assessments due, a population poll was taken every two years in which all the possessions of the subjects were also noted in addition to the number of family members who had reached full age. However, even before reaching maturity at eighteen years of age, the youth was required to pay his share of taxes; at thirteen, which was apparently the border between being a child and a young worker, the youth had to pay 3 *sho* a year (Brauen 1974, 165ff).

Distinctions between taxes whose payment was compulsory, and donations to monasteries were hazy; the eight government tax-paying families had regularly made an offering every year to a nearby monastery; When the monastery was taken over by the administration of another, larger monastery, the new administration confused the existing relationships of that county to the monastery, and saw in the freely given donation a required tax that was always to be paid. During the time of the former village headman, serious conflict had broken out over this misunderstanding. This regular, freely given donation was called *dad 'bul*, "religious offering". It is possible then, that some taxes had their beginnings in the generosity of the population. A tax respite existed theoretically but none of the villagers could remember ever having witnessed one.

The job of work that the governmental subjects actually had to do for the government was that of transport. Since the the thirteenth Dalai Lama the community had been rewarded for this service (Brauen 1974, 161). Whenever a governmental caravan, or someone carrying papers (*lam yig*) issued by the government, arrived at one of the two stations (*sa tshig*) that were at the boundaries of the researched area, then the community of governmental tax-payers had to send the requested number of beasts of burden or horses to carry them forward. The distance between two stations was normally about 14 English miles. For this distance the government paid two *sho* for each yak, or donkey and four *sho* for each horse, to the community of the governmental subjects. Foreigners, mainly Indians or Englishmen, paid one Rupee for a horse and half that for a yak or donkey. Besides the pack animals and saddle horses, the tax-payers also had to provide attendants for the caravan. The transport team was often accompanied by a younger brother who acted as a guide and was helped by a few paid workmen or tenants.

Along with the other two categories of subjects, the governmental tax-payers had also to take part in the construction of public roads and bridges. Since only one worker was required from each family for the public work, they were free to send a paid worker or tenant in their place.

Inheritance Laws:

In Tibetan the word "inheritance" is rendered by the word *pha zhi* (literally "fatherground") = "ground inherited from father". As suggested in the translation, this term is primarily to be understood as the farmland, along with the house, inherited from the father, in other words real estate. It should be remembered that, excepting the house, the "right to use" the land is meant by possession. The movable possessions of the family consisted for the main part of herds of stock, stored food, valuable garments, jewelry and gold.

The inheritance regulations were important for the governmental tax-payers because, along with the farm, the status of a governmental tax-payer was passed down to the eldest son. The brothers of the heir were then to enter a polyandric marriage with him in order to keep the whole of the land within the family for many generations. The sisters received their portions of movable goods and married men who were themselves heirs. If the brothers were not satisfied with the arrangement then they were paid off with movable goods; this happened when, for example, the second son decided to lead a monastic life and the third son loaned himself out as a caravan guide or shepherd and could not come to an understanding with the shared wife.

When, however, the eldest son was not capable of taking over the management of the farm, then the next son or the eldest daughter (when there were only female offspring) replaced him as heir. A female heir then married a man who became a member of her family and worked for them. The disinheritance of a son could only occur, when not only his family, but all of the governmental tax-payers were convinced that he was not qualified to carry the responsibility of a household. When this occurred, the son was provided with a bachelor's home for himself. If the late father, though not a subject of the government, had also married into a governmental tax-paying category of subjects and the mother possessed the land, then the eldest daughter automatically inherited the farm. The Tibetan economic system also shows here definite unilinear tendencies although kinsmanship was always interpreted as being bilateral.

The Tenants' Economic Situation - Lease and Property

The land that was owned by the community of governmental tax-payers as well as that which was privately owned by subjects of the government was leased partially to tenants (*dud chung*). According to the sources available to me, a tentative ratio of 1:2 may be assigned to the number of tax-paying householders in relationship to the number of settled tenants; paid workers and servants could not be taken into consideration, because they did not own their own homes.

The regulations concerning the leasing contract were of central importance to the farming community of Tibet. There were two types of tenure:

1. One received the land in exchange for a fixed amount of manual labour that was related to the size of the land. This type of lease was called a 'working lease' (*las zhing*)
2. One rented the land in exchange for a fixed amount of grain that also was determined according to the size of the land.

In the last decades the lease had been increasingly paid in cash. Fallow land was mainly leased under this type of agreement.

The poorer families usually entered into the "working lease" contract. The proprietor provided them with a small house, or a living apartment in his own home and a ration of one *ta'o*[4] about 3.4 kg of grain per day. The tenant also received three free meals on those days that he worked for the owner of the farm. Strictly considered, these tenants had two kinds of working conditions: firstly they were farmhands or herdsmen on the farm of their patron and secondly, they were small-time farmers themselves. Since this relationship included the whole family, some prosperity could be won from the work of all its members. The husband took the responsibility of being - for instance - a farmhand for the proprietor for six weeks; in exchange he received a piece of land requiring 21 *ta'o* (ca 71.5 kg) of seed, the 21 *ta'o* of seed, and 1 *ta'o* of grain a day which was altogether 42 *ta'o* (142.8 kg) of grain while he worked for his patron. In the time he had left over, he and his wife tilled and sowed the ground assigned to them. Their sons worked as shepherds for the patron as soon as they were ten years of age and the family was then usually entitled to free pasturage for their sheep. That the tenant did not have to pay duty on the yield of his farm, the animals he bred or his salary was a special advantage for the family. The "working lease" created a very strong bond between the proprietor or patron and the tenant, and in cases of misfortune the patron had to stand by the tenant and, if necessary, help him. In exchange for his greater dependency on the patron, the tenant received stronger social and economic protection.

However, this "working lease" was less common among the subjects of the government than the pecuniary leasing system.

The leasing of land for a sum of money implied a certain economic independance of the settler. He had to have a large enough reserve to provide for the difficult times that could come. The money leasing arrangement was usually made by families that had lived for a longer time in the county and who had a larger amount of property at their disposal.

Under the "working lease" relationship, a member of the tenant's family worked on the proprietor's field one day a year in exchange for a field that required one *ta'o* (ca. 3,4 kg) of seed. According to information received from my sources, a field that required 21 *ta'o* of seed was large enough for a small family. Since the fields of the tenants also yielded on the average five times the seed sown, a small family usually had ca. 357 kg of grain a year at their disposal, in which the daily grain allotment of the patron is not included.

Under the pecuniary system of leasing, between 25 and 30 *srang* a year were paid for a piece of land that required 20 *khal* (270 kg) of seed. In 1950 this sum of money was valued at 1½ *khal* of grain and since one can expect 100 *khal* of grain to be harvested from 20 *khal* of seed, the annual rent composed only 1 - 2% of the harvest. Most of the tenants had an annual rent of 30 - 50 *srang* to pay. In addition to this fee for the land was the money for pasturage, a charge for using the threshing floor, etc., so that the sum total of all debts came to be about 150 *srang* per year. The low lease charged was based upon the fact that most land rented under the pecuniary system was fallow land which the tenant would make into workable fields.

The possession of farmland was dependent upon the working capacity of the family and the amount of lease required, most tenants (*dud chung*) owned fields that needed 20 - 30 *khal* (270-405 kg) of seed.

The animals owned by the tenants were private and not associated with any kind of return service. Poor tenants owned 20 - 30 sheep as compared to the wealthier tenants who had up to 300 sheep. Aside from the few families that did not own any animals at all, the large majority of the tenants owned many sheep, a few cows, and one or two donkeys. The tenants possessed, however, no right to pastureland so that they had to ask their patron for permission to graze their animals. Pasture money (*rtsa rin*) was paid for this permission. Some were able to avoid this in that one or two members of the family, usually boys from ten to fifteen years of age, worked as shepherds for the patron. Free pasture usage was then included in their salaries.

The economic situation of the tenants could not be generalized too far; there were certainly some who had to get by with a very modest standard of living, but on the other side, the majority of the tenants were to a certain degree fairly satisfied with their situations. The patron offered them effective social and economic protection in cases of conflict and guaranteed them an adequate basis for existence with little responsibility. The fact that the tenants (*dud chung*) did not have to pay taxes of obligatory service like the tax-paying governmental, noble and monastic subjects did, was always considered to their advantage. They were only obliged to work on the construction of public roads and bridges.

The Economy of the Noble Estate

The Estate:
There was only one noble estate within the border of the county; the whole of this property was situated north of the monastic village on both sides of the river that flowed through the valley. The subjects of the noble landlord settled down in two different hamlets adding up to the village itself, which was located on the western shore of the river. The huge manor, which consisted of the house, the adjoining buildings, and the surrounding fields, lay a little down river on the opposite shore. Next

Plate 5. When the cultivation of land starts, the animals drawing the plough are decorated with ribbons and tassels.

to the manor was the resting station for the governmental couriers (*'a drung*). There was, however, no connection between the courier station and the estate.

The noble manor was the landed property of an aristocratic family that had been in the service of the government for centuries. It was said that the fifth Dalai Lama (1617-1682) had rewarded the family for loyal service with a grant of this land. Over the centuries they had acquired further properties but this estate remained the largest. The proceeds of this estate and others served as remuneration for the service to the state.[5] Along with this fief was given the right to demand service or corvée (Johnson 1960, 205) from the tenants under the noble family's administration. In return the government freed the tenants largely from any payment of taxes in goods. The only remaining obligation then was to provide one soldier out of a certain number of subjects and to do the compulsory work on public roads and bridges.

In the last three decades this particular noble family had included three brothers, two of whom stood in the service of the State and lived in Lha-sa. The middle brother oversaw the administration of the different estates from his residence in the nearby city. He was also responsible for the noble estate in the researched area.

The farmland of the noble estate covered an area requiring 500 *khal* (6750 kg) of seed. The quality of soil was for the most part middling, so that one could normally expect a yield of five times the amount of seed sown. Accordingly, the estate must have produced about 33,750 kg of grain a year. In addition to this, the estate also owned extensive pasture land on the mountains that surrounded the valley. Altogether the estate administered three sheep farms with seven sheep herds and owned a large yak and *'bri* herd. Because the pasturage owned by the estate, in spite of its extent, was not enough for all the sheep, land was also rented from the community of governmental tax-payers (*khral pa spyi pa*).

The farms and herds of the noblemen were cared for by their tenants. For their farm labour, they were given a piece of land that was only remotely related in size to the amount of service rendered. Those tenants who were engaged as shepherds, received the herd under tightly fixed conditions. The percentage of the products to be delivered - butter, yoghurt, cheese, wool, meat - were written in the tax records of the manor. These herdsmen had no further taxes to pay.

Since tenants were obliged to pay tribute to the lord of the manor, those who possessed large properties were also called *khral pa*, "tax-payers". There was, however, a considerable difference from the category of the governmental tax-payers: Tax-payers of the government produced goods on their own lands and at their own direction, the tax thereof was then all delivered collectively on the specified day of the year. On the other hand, the tax-payer subjugated to the nobility paid his tribute through labour and at the direction of the overseer. The governmental subject considered himself "free" and the subject of the noble estate felt oppressed and in bondage. My decision to call the small farmers subjected to the noble land-lord "tenant" and to restrict the term "tax-payer" to the two stewards and some other noble subjects who owned large properties and herds was based upon this distinction. By this means only noble subjects with large farms and numerous herds were called like the governmental subjects, "tax-payers", while all the other noble subjects were called "tenants" as the *dud chung*, the client of a governmental tax-payer was already named.

In determining the labour obligation, the mathematical unit *rkang* was used as a basic unit; one *rkang* was the equivalent of six **phu-lu*. Within the category of subjects of the nobility one **phu-lu* designated half the work capacity of a man, so that a work team of one *rkang* consisted of three fully capable men. A distinction was made between *phyi rkang*, those who worked outside the house and *nang rkang*, those who worked inside it.[6] An assessment of property in **phu-lu* as occurred under the governmental tax-payers was not known by the subjects of the nobility. The estate management reckoned on so many *rkang* from a certain settlement. In other words, all the tenant farmers who lived in settlement A had collectively to supply the manor with a certain number of work groups (*rkang*), irrespective of the actual number of tenants. When the number of men capable of working did not cover the number of *rkang* demanded, substitutes (*khral skyor*) were engaged. The reaching of maturity was unimportant under this economic structure, as the labour duty was a fixed rate for the household as a whole.

For the single tenant family this usually meant that one group (*rkang*) had to be kept ready for the landlord's use. A normal family that consisted of a couple, the parents and a few children was therewith already pushed to the limits of its capacity. If, as in the case of the tenants of the upper settlements, additional responsibilities to the government were also added, then either a very large family or many paid workers were needed in order to cope with the task. The majority of the tenants of the upper settlement were also obliged to provide a further work group (*rkang*) for the government.

When a family split up, because, for example, the parents and their married children could not get along together, then the tax obligations were divided between them. In this way a tenant from the lower settlement who lived only with his wife and one small child had to provide two *phu-lu*, i.e. 1/3 *rkang* or one worker; whereas the whole family together, that had included the parents of the man and his brothers and sisters, had had to provide a complete work group of three persons for the noble estate.

When a tenant became 60 years of age, he was freed from duty, but was still allowed to remain on the tenant farm. His children took over his duties and cared for their old parents. If the couple had had no children of their own, then they looked for children that might be up for adoption among their relatives; the landlord also provided adoptive children in some cases. The adopted children then worked the farm and provided for the payment of taxes. With the death of the old parents, the adopted children inherited the farm as their own and entered then the same dependent relationship to the noble landlord as that of the parents. The reaching of seniority, then, was only important for the individual; it had no effect on the household of the tenant farmer.

Some well-to-do tenants hired labourers who were responsible only to the tenant even when working for him on the lands of the noble estate. The manor overseer had absolutely no authority over these workers and they had no taxes to pay or duty to fulfil. The same was also true of the paid herdsmen who worked under the direction of the chief shepherd. These herdsmen had private working contracts whose conditions were arranged between the two parties involved.

The Management of the Noble Estate:

Theoretically the whole estate was controlled only by the noble family; in practice, however, the system of power distribution had also established itself here. The nobleman delegated authority to a prominent servant on his estate; he was placed in the office of *phyag mdzod* - literally translated "treasure-keeper", and the treasurer functioned in much the same way as a landlord. This *phyag mdzod* had the real authority on the estate; he made all the important decisions in the name of his lord. The nobleman often did not even bother with his estate or was not in a position to do so. The power of the *phyag mdzod* was most revealed by the fact that the highest judge on the noble estate was the *phyag mdzod* and not the noble himself. The next higher judicial institute was that of the government, represented by the district governor (*rdzong dpon*); the lower judicial institute was the manager or steward of the estate (*gzhi gnyer pa* or *gzhi sdod pa*). The *phyag mdzod* usually resided in the same place as the noble in the area researched, the *phyag mdzod* only visited the estate on specific occasions, for instance, always during the sheep shearing season, otherwise he stayed with the lord of the manor in Gyantse.

Under the *phyag mdzod* were two stewards (*gzhi sdod pa*). One of them lived in the large old manor and was responsible for the manor and the lower settlement. Both of them together determined the daily schedule of the estate. They divided the work among the tenant work groups (*rkang*) and oversaw the execution of the work. They provided the tools, seed, beast of burden and field implements, and were responsible for collecting the tax-goods — especially from the shepherds. For this task the steward had his "tax-book" (*ma deb*) in which all debts were recorded. Outside these areas the authority of a steward was very limited. When a tenant was lazy at his work, then the steward could reprimand him and as the heaviest disciplinary punishment he could box his ears. All other physical punishments were reserved for the lord or the *phyag mdzod*. Yet the steward had an important function in social life; he mediated in the numerous squabbles and conflicts that arose among the tenants. Since he belonged, however, to the same social rank as those subordinate to him, tensions resulting from differences between ranks hardly every occurred. In fact, the stewards were often the friends and confidants of the tenants. In the social structure of the noble estate, the stewards functioned as neutralizers and emotional stabilizers. On the other hand, an efficient and hard working steward was essential, which greatly enhanced the position of the steward in conflicts with the nobility[7].

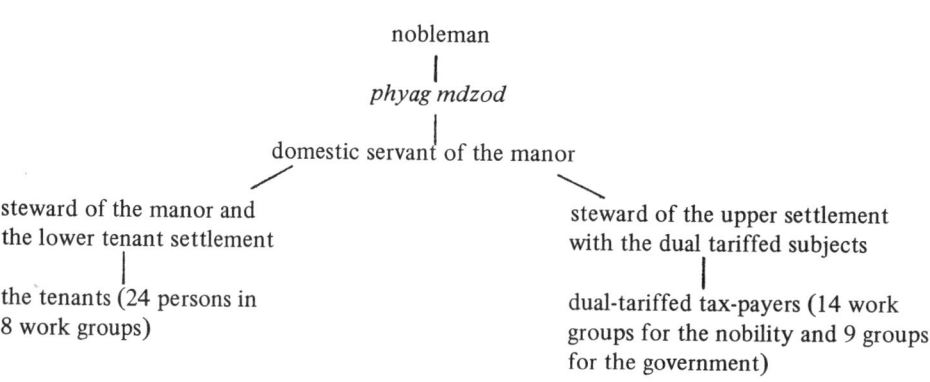

Organisation of the Noble Estate

The Lower Settlement:
Besides the subjects of the nobility, one or two families lived in the lower settlement who were subjects of the government and one further family was subject to the monastery. These exceptional cases had no economic or other institutionalized relationships with the noble estate.

The estate land belonging to the lower settlement required 180 *khal* (2430 kg) of seed. The average yearly yield was five-fold, about 900 *khal* (12,150 kg). Barley was the most important grain grown, but at the lower settlement of the estate peas were also cultivated. These did not grow in other parts of the valley. Three teams of animals, i.e. six beasts, were at the disposal of the tenants for tillage. These animals had earlier also been cared for by the tenants but the steward took possession of them under the "no birth - no death" system explained above. Three further teams of animals were provided for the upper settlement.

The noble estate owned eight herds of sheep, each of which was cared for by a shepherd who had a sheepfarm in the middle of the pasture land; these houses were called *sa tshig*, not to be mistaken for the postal stations which were called the same. When the sheep were driven further afield to graze, then the shepherds lived in tents. In all other aspects the shepherd's household was exactly like that of the villagers who lived in the valley. These shepherds often hired men to help them with their work. Two herds were pastured together and comprised a *lug khag, that could include up to 3000 sheep. According to unanimous testimony, the sheep herds were so large, they "covered the mountain sides like snow". In addition to these extensive herds, the noble estate owned a yak and *'bri* herd of 121 animals.

The tenants of the lower settlement had collectively to provide 24 persons in eight working groups for the estate. The field work began in winter with the fertilization of the land. Ploughing sowing, and harrowing followed in the second month of the Tibetan year, mostly around March. During the main growing season the fields had to be watered and weeded; in autumn the crops were harvested. Since waggons or carts pulled either by animals or humans were hardly ever found in Tibet, the harvest was loaded on the backs of yaks or donkeys who brought the grain to the threshing places. If the field was too difficult for the animal to reach, or if the farmer had no beasts of burden, then the grain had to be carried on his back. Pack baskets and barrows used for this task are very similar to those still used in the Alps today. These are also to be found in the Tibetan refugee camps in India. The grain was threshed on a platform reserved for this task near the estate manor. Yak and 'bri were prodded to tread the sheaves of grain which were then thrown against the wind to separate the chaff from the wheat. In doing so some of the tenants always tried to leave a certain part of the grain in the chaff because this was then treated as refuse and they could later collect the grain for themselves. Because this happened often, the practice of posting one of the overseers of the estate to control the threshing and check the chaff was established. When he found too much grain in the chaff the steward was held responsible. The grain was then measured and stored at the manor until it was to be sold or lent out.

All the tenants were needed as land labourers (*zhing g-yog*) for a series of days to fertilize the ground in the winter, to till the fields in the spring and to harvest the crops in the autumn. Only a few work groups were needed in between for watering and weeding the crops. The distribution of the groups and their work was the responsibility of the steward. The work and tax to be paid was checked against the "tax-book" (*ma deb*) of the steward. The amount of taxes to be paid and service to be done was a fact of life for the villagers, so they did not worry about its origin. No one could remember when the last tax assessment had been defined; it seems however to have been determined at the end of the last century or the beginning of this (Brauen 1974, 142; Shakabpa 1967, 113 n. 20).

The compulsory work on the estate of the nobleman was called '*u lag*, a term that usually designates only the transport obligation when it is found in literature (Brauen 1974, 161; SCD 1115). The settlers further specified their work as being that of land labourers (*zhing g-yog*).

The actual extent of this compulsory work is difficult to determine. Some informants complained that they were forced to work in the fields from dawn to dusk; others still found time to take on an extra job for which they were paid.[8] The individual circumstances make objective situations appear in an ever changing light. However, it was noticeable that most of the larger families had to provide one working group of three persons for the estate.

Sheep raising on the estate was carried out through the leasing of the herd. The shepherd considered the herd to be "his", although he knew very well that the herd had been given to his ancestors by the noble estate. Nevertheless, the shepherd carried full responsibility for the herd. Thus the appearance of disease among the animals was no concern of the landed nobility at all; regardless of the actual size of the herd, the shepherd had to deliver a set amount of produce that was based on the theoretical figures recorded in the tax-book (*ma deb*) of the steward. Differences between the actual amount that the herd could produce and what was recorded in this little book had to be paid in cash by the shepherd.

The system by which sheep reproduction was officially reckoned was called "three ewes, two lambs" (*ma gsum bu gnyis*). The most important regulations of this system are such: 1/12 of the whole herd was subtracted each year as the death rate, the remainder was then divided in two, signifying the division of male and female sheep. The number of ewes was divided by three; two thirds of which were considered pregnant. This number of ewes was then the basis of the butter that had to be delivered each year; 4 *nya ga* (i.e. 2.7 kg), later 5 *nya ga* (3.37 kg) of butter per ewe per year was claimed by the noble estate.

The skin of an animal that had died was to be delivered to the landlord and the head to the steward; the flesh was given to a tenant who promised in return to plait a certain amount of yak hair into cord and weave a certain amount of wool into cloth, which was then all to be delivered to the estate. To determine the amount of wool yielded, the sheep were divided into age groups; a lamb was first shorn at two years of age when a lesser amount of wool was expected. The wool was taken to the manor and received by the *phyag mdzod*, representing the landlord. All wool produced belonged to the noble estate.

One of the former stewards offered to write down from memory the entries used for assessing the herds of sheep. The starting herd count and the name of the shepherd are his inventions but, the rations, and all the technical terms are true to the original method. The full text of his tax list is included in the appendix. These entries were continued year after year, always based upon the latest count of the herd. Based upon this testimony, the following reproduction coefficients were established: When "a" is the number of sheep in the original herd, then the reproduction of that herd will be $\frac{11}{36}$ a. From this the following equations may be set up:

Head of sheep during the first year calculated: $a + \frac{11}{36}a = a_1$

Head of sheep during the second year of calculation: $a_1 + \frac{11}{36}a_1 = a_2$ and so on.

Shepherds that I questioned knew nothing about the care of sick animals. Sheep raising was considered only by numbers and never by the yield of the individual animal. The animals were not fed in winter, the shepherds drove them to snow-free meadows where they were kept in pens. Weak or sick animals usually did not survive; the healthy animals were but skin and bones by springtime. In spite of these hard conditions, none of the Tibetan informants reported high death rates among the animals. Epidemics apparently only rarely occurred.

There were two different systems for the leasing of large stock herds. The first was similar to that used for sheep with the difference that the *'bri* was calculated to have calved only every second year. Thus, the reproduction of a herd in the original year of calculation is $\frac{11}{48}a$ and the herd consisted of a + $\frac{11}{48}a = a_1$ animals. The second method of large-stock leasing was the "no birth-no death" system (*skyes med 'chi med*) whereby the sum total of animals in the herd remained constant, as was the amount of butter and cheese to be delivered to the estate. The actual increase or decrease of stock was the profit or loss of the shepherd.

The large yak and *'bri* herds of the noble estate had been originally given out under the first system explained above, later they were leased under the "no birth-no death" system whereby certain exceptions were made: 21 *'bri* from 121 animals had (theoretically) to calve per year. Seven calves were then given to the shepherd as remuneration for his services; the equivalent of fourteen calves was to be paid to the estate in cash. One calf was worth 5 *rdo tshad*. For each of the 21 *'bri* the shepherd was further to deliver 2 *khal* (27 kg) of butter. The *'bri* that did not calve were called *yar ma*, "barren". One *khal* and ten *nya ga* (20.25 kg) of butter was to be paid for each of these barren *'bri*. Altogether the herdsman was to deliver 88 *khal* (1,180 kg) of butter a year, or substitute 5 *rdo tshad* for each *khal*. The market price in the county for one *khal* of butter was 6 *rdo tshad*. Cheese was also to be handed over for each *'bri*. The total sum was 15 *'bo* (8.25 l.) of grated cheese; 30 *'bo* (16.5 l.) of dried cheese slices; and 30 *'bo* (16.5 l.) of salted cheese cubes.[9]

The wool of yak and *'bri* was separated into soft underwool (*khu lu*) and long, stiff outer hair. The herdsman was to deliver 4 *nya ga* (22 l.) of underwool and 4 *nya ga* (22 l.) of outer hair from each animal.

The herdsman who had looked after the yak and *'bri* herd also gave some information about the care and handling of sick animals. The only animal epidemic that he knew of was called *glo nad* and occurred when he was still a young boy. Which disease it was remains unfortunately undefined.[10] When an animal caught this disease it was bled and its blood was mixed with water to form a type of serum. This was poured into the mouths of the other animals in the herd as a liquid vaccination (*kan rtsi*). The treated animal suffered from the *glo nad* disease for a couple of days after which it was immune. The blood of the animals that had been vaccinated in this way could then be used for further vaccinations.[11]

In winter, the yak and *'bri* also remained outside and grazed on grass that had been cleared of snow by the wind. They seldom froze to death, and never caught diseases except the *glo nad* epidemic mentioned above.

Butter production was described as follows by the informant responsible for it. The *'bri* were milked in the morning and the warm milk was cooled in a cold water bath. At midday the milk was reheated and poured into a wooden butter churn. The separation of buttermilk and butter was accomplished by the pumping of the wooden rod.[12] Yoghurt was prepared from goat and sheep milk. If the butter was to be stored for the winter it was immediately sewn into pieces of damp leather after if had been very carefully processed so as not to leave any water in it. The leather package was then set in the sun for a short while so that the air inside the package was forced out by the fast drying and shrinking of the leather. The butter was well conserved through this process, it was then stored in cool caverns until autumn, when it was brought back to the valley.

Cheese too was an important part of the Tibetan diet. To make it sour milk was heated until the water was separated from the solid ingredients. Every drop of moisture had to be squeezed out from the curd which was then shaped into little balls or cutlets. They were put into the bright sunlight to get completely dry. If some cheese was required for cooking the hard cheese-cutlet was ground up and put into soups; it was sometimes also mixed with Tsampa, butter and sugar to make *thud*, a kind of sweet. As Tibetan cheese was never salted or spiced, it might be more correct to call it dried curd rather than cheese.

The Upper Settlement:

The following history was pieced together from the information collected. The whole settlement, including subjects, had once belonged only to the government and the inhabitants were governmental tax-payers with the same status as that of the corresponding group in the county until recently. Since the noblemen who owned the estate in this county needed more workers than lived in the lower settlement, the government granted permission for him to acquire further settlers as tenants. However, the government could not afford to give up a whole settlement without due recompense and so a compromise was reached. The inhabitants of the upper settlement had to provide fourteen work groups (*rkang*) i.e. forty-two land labourers [13] for the noble landlord and nine work groups, twenty-seven persons, for the government transport service (Brauen 1974, 161); two of these groups had to house officials whenever they came and pay 25 *srang* for the couriers' food. The nine work groups serving the government, including the two who sheltered the couriers, took turns in the fulfilment of these duties. The law determining how many workers one particular family had to supply of the total 14 working groups had long been established and was not dependent upon the number of members in that family. These inhabitants of the upper settlement were called "dual-tariffed" tax-payers.

All the resident families of the dual-tariffed category had approximately the same amount of land, namely that which required 150 *khal* (2025 kg) of seed.[14] Some families owned more pasturage, others more farmland. Some of the families could not work all of their land because they lacked adequate manpower. Since the land had all been originally leased to the subjects from the government, they received no acreage from the nobility. The noble landlord owned a tract of land that required 160 *khal* (2160 kg) of seed, other than this he did not own any further land in this particular settlement.

All rights and responsibilities based upon the possession of this land especially as regards the simultaneous membership in two categories of subjects, as well as exactly defined land boundaries were recorded in a document. These regulations were apparently clear and practical in application as all informants unanimously agreed that there had never been any disagreements or misunderstandings concerning them.

The taxes of the inhabitants of the upper settlement consisted of the provision of labour forces as described above and the following natural goods: five sheep, equivalent to 18 *khal* (243 kg) of meat and a certain amount of butter (the informants could no longer remember the exact amount). These goods were then given to the government by the landlord.

Additionally the dual-tariffed tax-payers had to raise the so-called "military tax" (*dmag khral*). The exact stipulation varied depending upon the political situation; earlier, 14 work groups had had to provide one fully equipped soldier; later every six work groups had had to send a soldier; then it was declared that 15 groups were collectively to provide three soldiers for the army. When none of the settlers were willing to volunteer for the army, they tried to convince a hired worker to do so: when that didn't work either, they tried to make a soldier's life seem attractive to a tramp or traveller in the area. The tax-payers then had to provide all the soldier's equipment and his wages.

Since the inhabitants of the upper settlement served two landlords simultaneously, the provision of workers for both sometimes resulted in an overlap of duty. For example, if a family had to send three workers to the fields of the nobleman and a governmental transport happened to come at the same time, the family was overburdened and could no longer supply the manpower for all the tasks demanded of it. Since none of the duties could be postponed (a clear characteristic of *'u lag* work) the family had to ask neighbours for help. One of them then fulfilled some of the duties which naturally had the consequence of obliging them to help him in similar situations. The overlapping of two opposing duties is the original for the institutionalisation of the readiness to help which is so characteristic of the whole social sphere of the Tibetan rural population. Their economic situation resulted in a willingness to help each other which is presupposed by a conflict-free relationship between neighbours which is again typical of Tibetan society. One could rely upon people who professionally took over tax-duties (*khral skyor*): however it seems that there were actually not very many of them.

The Tenants and Their Way of Life:

Besides the service and tribute owed to the noble landlord, the settlers also had taxes to pay that went to the state or the county. The transport duty, already mentioned above in connection with the dual-tariffed tax-payers of the upper settlement, was also requested from all the other tenants of the other categories. When a courier or caravan arrived at the station carrying official travelling papers (*lam yig*), five horses had to be sent to accompany him to the next station. The subjects of the noble estate had to provide nine groups (*rkang*) for transport service and the whole county supplied 38 such groups in total. All inhabitants of the county, including the tenants of the noble estate, were required to work on public roads and bridges.

The tenants of the lower settlement had also to supply 24 beasts of burden for a special transport from the neighbouring county into their own; this special duty was called *um-phu.

Those members of the family that had originally been subjects of another landlord but had then married into this county, had to pay a "man-tax" (*mi bogs*) of a few *srang* a year to their old landlord.

With regard to the possibility of a tax respite, the informants were of different opinions. The landlord said that a tax respite was possible in the event of a general catastrophe for example a bad harvest, hail etc.. The settlers, however, and the stewards of the estate denied the possibility of a tax respite. The cause of the conflict in opinion seems to have been the term "general catastrophe". For the estate nobleman this term meant a vast natural catastrophe and since the settlers had never experienced this, they were not aware that a tax respite was possible. One must further consider that most

Plate 6. A Tibetan farmer harrowing with decorated draught animals.

Plate 7. Domestic animals treading out grain on the threshing floor.

of the tax on the noble estate was in the form of compulsory work and so could not be deferred anyway. The secondary taxes which included natural goods were so small that every tenant could afford to borrow from his neighbours in order to produce the tax.

Only the herdsmen had to supply large amounts of agricultural products that were reckoned mathematically and not according to the actual produce of the herds. If the assessments could not be fully paid in a certain year, then the herdsmen had to borrow enough money to be able to pay the difference in cash; there was no interest charged on the debt. Only in exceptional cases could the tax owed be paid in the following year. If one of the tenants needed grain, which was also used as money, he could borrow small amounts from the steward of the estate and larger amounts from the *phyag mdzod*. Ten percent interest was charged a year for the grain loan. For a settler who had borrowed grain outside his own category of subjects, interest of 20 - 25% was not uncommon. The ten per cent interest was held to be a privilege of the nobility subjects.

Money that was borrowed also incurred an interest of ten per cent a year; meat and butter were never lent, as they were not considered essential for life.

Subjects of the noble estate received their homes from the noble landlord. They were simply built of stone with a stall and sometimes a hay loft on the ground floor; the upper floor was mainly taken up by the kitchen (*thab tshang*) that functioned as a living and sleeping area for all members of the family, sometimes a pantry was connected to it. In the lower settlement only the three-storied house of the estate steward had over ten rooms. However, most were used for storage.

The dual-tariffed tax-payers of the upper settlement in general owned larger and better furnished homes that they or their forefathers had built themselves. The herdsmen usually had to build their own houses in the pasture-land. These houses had several storage rooms for cheese, butter, etc. In all cases the land on which the houses stood belonged to the landlord; however, there was no lease to be paid on this land in contrast to the governmental tax-payers.

The landed property of the settlers varied greatly in size but in general the tenants of the lower settlement owned a field that required 3 - 4 *khal* (40.5 - 54 kg) of seed. The steward had originally owned no more land than the others; as his seven children grew up and the field could no longer feed a family of eleven members, he had had to lease fallow land from the noble landlord and additional fields from the monastery. He paid 6 - 7 *khal* (81 - 94.5 kg) of butter a year for this monastery land. Converted to money this butter was worth about 36 to 42 *rdo tshad*, or 1800 to 2100 *srang*, or 12 to 14 *khal* grain in the 1950's. Altogether the steward had ten fields but he could not remember the amount of seed needed for them.

The dual-tariffed tax-payers of the upper settlement owned land that, if one had sown the entire area, would have required 150 *khal* (2025 kg) of grain. Next to the governmental tax-payers, they owned the largest farms in the whole country.

Generally the tenants of the lower settlement owned fewer animals than those of the upper settlement. The animals that they did have were their own private possessions. When the tenant had no pasturage himself he had to rent it either for money or for butter. Some even managed to make good deals: the stewards, like the herdsmen, could pasture their animals in the meadows of the noble estate for free.

The smallest family of the lower settlement, consisting of a couple and a small child, owned no more than one cow and a donkey. The steward of the lower settlement owned ten cows, four yaks and *'bri*, two horses and twenty to thirty sheep. The chief herdsman of the noble estate, however, had even more - along with his ten head of large stock he also possessed 300 sheep and goats.

Most of the tenants in the upper settlement owned two to five cows, a few donkeys and between fifty and two hundred sheep. They were all supposed to have at least one horse for governmental transport but actually only a few of those questioned had really owned a horse. When they needed one, they preferred to borrow it as that was less expensive in the long run than owning one themselves; horses were not so useful on a farm as yaks.

The tenants' own private harvests on their land insured the livelihood of the whole family. They were not taxed on the crops of their own farms. Added to this was a fixed reimbursement for the work done on the estate. The steward received for example, 12 *khal* (162 kg) of grain a year from the noble landlord, 17 *khal* (229, 5 kg) grain from the settlers under him, and a certain amount of meat;[15] besides this, his fields were worked by the tenants of the noble estate and he could use the pasture-land free for his animals. The reimbursement of tenants for their services was 24 *khal* (324 kg) of grain paid per year collectively to every work group (*rkang*). Tenants and dual-tariffed tax-payers of the upper settlement received the fees from transport service as additional income. These were the same as those paid to the governmental tax-payers. Shepherds and herdsmen received a percentage of the herd increase per year: for example the yak herder received seven calves per year and the shepherd all those lambs over two thirds the number of ewes. The yak herder could lend his animals out for transport or for threshing grain. From this income he had leased a field in the valley that needed ten *khal* (135 kg) of seed; his friends there worked on his field as well as their own for which he provided them with as much butter as they wanted. One further important source of income for the herdsmen was in selling dried yak and sheep dung for fuel. One load of yak dung brought 30 *srang*, that of sheep dung, 20 *srang*.

The shepherds could not lend out their animals as beasts of burden but they received between 40 and 60 *khal* (540 - 810 kg) of grain instead, the exact amount being determined by the size of the herd.

A summary of the economic situation of the subjects of the noble estate results in the following picture:

The tenants of the lower settlement could only just manage to feed themselves with their small fields. Only with much hard work could they succeed in saving up for a better living standard. Since there was only one known case of a tenant being able to rise from being a mere subject of the nobility into the somewhat better situation of a dual-tariffed tax-payer, one may assume that the limited acreage of the lower settlement only barely sufficed and that few took on the extra trouble of saving up to move into the upper settlement through doing additional work under the dual-tariffed tax-payers. If, on the other hand, it had been impossible to rise to the status of a dual-tariffed tax-payer, and if the private fields had not produced enough to live on, there would have certainly been more cases of families secretly running away - as two herder families apparently had done - although no one would comment on this.

The tenants and dual-tariffed tax-payers of the upper settlement were rightly called "large-scale" farmers; they owned extensive land which also made it possible for them to hire workers as their substitutes on the fields of the noble estate. These farmers were wealthy because, as mentioned above, the transport services also provided extra income.

The herdsmen could usually manage their herds at a profit, though it was sometimes difficult for the yak herdsmen to raise the money to find the butter tribute due, in addition to the money for the fourteen calves (70 *rdo tshad*).

None of the subjects of the nobility would - given the possibility to do so - have wanted to return to the life that they had lived before the flight from Tibet. The reason however, was not the economic circumstances that prevailed because some of them are much worse off since leaving, but rather the unsatisfying social positions that they had been in.

Inheritance Laws:

As in the other social categories, the land and home were together called *pha gzhi* ("father-ground") by the subjects of the nobility. It had been lent out by the landlord and so the inheritance laws were determined by those concerning the transference of the dependency from father to son. These stipulations will be mentioned here briefly again. When the father was a subject of the nobility and the marriage was patrilocal, then the sons would also be subject of the noble estate and the eldest son usually inherited the farm. When the mother was a subject of the nobility and the marriage was matrilocal the eldest daughter would inherit the farm. The rest of the siblings could live and work on the farm as long as they were unmarried. They had to find a wife who would inherit her own farm.

Special positions among the tenants, for example the estate stewardship, could not be inherited. They were bestowed by the noble landlord according to the merit and ability of the tenant. The ablest of the sons of the old steward was often appointed, but none of the sons had a right to the office. The tenant status could never be taken away from a subject of the nobility by any move of the landlord; only the herdsmen could be dismissed when they had neglected the herd and not delivered the required taxes.

The Economy of the Monastic Estate (*chos gzhi*)

The monastery in this county was several centuries old and in the British-Tibetan war (1904) the temple had been largely destroyed. It was described by G. Tucci in detail, but discretion for the former inhabitants of the village forbids me doing so here. The aristocratic family that had its main estate in this county had established the monastery and donated the small estate that belonged to it. Since then the bond between the monastery and the nobleman had been very strong. The inhabitants of the monastery belonged to the dGe-lugs-pa school (Snellgrove/Richardson 1968, 177ff) which was also the school of the Dalai Lama. This monastery, along with fifteen other monasteries, was subordinate to the district administration in Gyantse. The different aspects of this dependency are not important for this examination and so will not be discussed in any more detail.

The monks lived from the harvest of the noble estate and the goods (butter, Tsampa, etc.). offered to them. Each monk belonging to the monastery, there were about 200 of them, received 16 *khal* (216 kg) of grain in the autumn after the harvest had been threshed; other allowances were donated by private patrons (*sbyin bdag*).

The monastic estate consisted of fields and pasturage; the size of the fields could no longer be determined exactly. Based upon the number of tenants needed to work the land, it seems to have been about half as large as that of the noble estate. Barley and peas were the crops grown there. Two herdsmen were enough to manage the two small pastures that also belonged to the monastery. The estate owned about 1000 sheep and 600 yak and *'bri*.

The Administration of the Monastic Estate:

There are certain similarities between the administrations of the noble and monastic estates. Neither the abbot nor any committee of monks were bothered with looking after the estate, this was the job of the *phyag mdzod* or *gnyer pa*, as he was also called. Subordinate to him were two stewards (*gzhi' sdod pa*) who were each responsible for half the estate's farmland. The pasturage was the direct responsibility of the *gnyer pa* and not one of the two stewards. The duties of the monastic stewards were similar to those of the noble estate; the only important difference between the two was that the fields of the monastic stewards were not worked on by the tenants as was the case of the noble estate.

There were twenty-four subjects who had inherited their bondage to the monastery; that means that when the mother was a member of these twenty-four subjects, then the eldest daughter inherited the dependency just as the oldest son followed the father. These twenty-four monastery subjects were also divided into work groups (*rkang*) of three persons each.

There were sixty additional subjects who had at some time voluntarily applied for work and security at the monastery; they had become subjects, but with the privilege of being able to cancel the dependency at any moment.

Monastic order

```
                          gnyer pa
                             |
                        two stewards
                        /          \
   twenty-four permanent subjects    sixty voluntary subjects
```

The lowest judicial court was that of the steward who settled small differences. Important cases were brought before the *gnyer pa* of the monastery; if, however, they concerned tilled land, then the "hail-protector" acted as mediator. The next higher court was a four person committee of the monastic administration, above this was a larger committee in which there was a representative of the monks, and the highest court was the district administration in Gyantse that was appealed to in serious criminal cases such as murder.

Taxes and Compulsory Service:

Field work was the only compulsory duty for subjects of the monastery. All tenants had to first work the monastic fields that were under one steward, and then the other steward's half. The steward appointed work groups (*rkang*) who took turns in the watering and weeding of the land. Two families were appointed to care exclusively for the governmental transports and were freed from further duties.

An individual subject was obliged to work for the monastery from his tenth to his sixtieth birthday. A ten year old, however, was not expected to fulfil the duties of a fully grown man; a boy from a wealthy family was expected to do half a man's work and a ten year old son of a poor family had to do one fourth of a full job.

Since most of the marriages were between different categories of subjects, i.e. exogamous, this individual determination of duty meant that usually only one of the parents had to do compulsory labour. Old parents that had not quite reached the age of sixty also did not have to work a full quota and no work was required from small children. These were the decisive advantages that the subjects of the monastery had; they themselves considered the division of work fair and flexible.

Information about the duties and taxes on the herdsmen was not available since no former herdsmen of the monastic estate could be interviewed. One may assume that in general the rules concerning the herds of the noble estate also applied to those of the monastery since none of the informants knew of any systems of animal lease other than the "no birth-no death"(*skyes med 'chi med*) and the "three ewes,two lambs"(*ma gsum bu gnyis*) methods.

Since no natural goods had to be paid as taxes to the monastery, tax respites were of no concern. Two *ta'o* of grain were charged for the loan of 25 *khal* of grain in order to meet the future shrinkage of the fresh grain that was returned instead of the old and fully dried grain originally given. This interest of 2% a year was called *skam chags*, "meeting the dryness". These rate were only valid for the monastic subjects; when subjects of other categories wanted to borrow grain from the monastery, they had to pay 10% interest per year. The highest interest rate in the county was the 20-25% a year that the governmental tax-payers demanded of the other social categories. Money was also borrowed from the monastery at 10% interest.

The Economic Situation of the Monastic Tenants:

Both the fields and meadows of the monastery were less extensive than those of the noble estate. The land was not leased to a family as a whole but instead was bound to the individual subject alone. Each subject had the use of a field that needed 6 *khal* (81 kg) of seed. The land was bestowed on the subject as soon as he became a full member, so that when there were several of these in one family (for example: grandmother, mother and a teenage daughter), the family simultaneously owned three fields each needing 6 *khal* (81 kg) of grain or, altogether, 18 *khal* (243 kg) of seed. One of the stewards of the monastery had farmlands of this size. On the other hand, a family might have had only one subject (for example: only the father since there was no son over 10 years of age and the grandfather had already died); such was the case of a carpenter and his family, they only owned one field needing 6 *khal* of grain. The sixty voluntary subjects had the same economic status as the permanent monastic subjects.

The possession of animals was also somewhat more limited than on the noble estate. Just as on that estate, the stewards owned more stock that the other tenants, above all many horses and yak. Stewards could freely use the estate pasturage for their animals. There were no taxes or duties on the settlers' possession of animals.

Because the land provided for the tenants was scanty, the monastery additionally gave them a portion of grain, 12 *khal* (162 kg) per subject per year. Half of this was distributed in the spring and half in the autumn, just after the threshing. Furthermore the tenants received free meals on the days that they worked the estate fields. The salaries of the stewards were 50 *khal* (675 kg) of grain each per year.

Many former villagers considered the subjects of the monastery equal in status to the governmental tax-payers, or even better, so that it is no wonder that half the subjects of the monastery that were questioned said that they would like to work under their old landlord again.

Inheritance Laws:

Since land possession was bound up with the status of subject, the land was inherited along with the dependency. As mentioned before, the dependency was passed on only unilinearly, i.e. from the father to usually the eldest son, and from the mother to the eldest daughter. The possessions of the parent who was not a subject of the monastery were transmitted according to the inheritance laws of that particular category of subjects.

General Duties of All Three Categories of Subjects

All residents had to maintain the state roads (*gzhung lam*) and bridges within the boundaries of county; when repairs were needed, each family had to send one worker. During this work the labourers received no food or any other kind of salary; the task was overseen and directed by the younger village headman (*rgan chung*). One other obligation that was mentioned by several informants needs further investigation, namely that of each family having to send one son to the monastery (*grva khral*) (Goldstein 1971 a, 20). This rule was supposed to apply to the governmental tax-payers and the wealthier tenants of the noble and the monastic estates. A prerequisite for applying this rule was the family having at least three sons. When this was the case the well-to-do families were supposed to send the second son, the poorer families the first son and the middle class families the third son to the monastery.

This practice seemed to have been long out of use because the large majority of families, when asked if there had been a monk in the family, answered in the negative although most of them had had more than three sons. To further questioning, the villagers explained that yes, there had been such a regulation, but that one didn't always have to follow it. It appears to have been an obsolete tax that was still remembered but never fulfilled. Only one third of those families who would have been subject to this obligation replied that they had a brother or son in a monastery; those children who are today in Indian monasteries are also included in this number. When one includes only the boys who actually become monks out of those who would have been affected by this rule, then the percentage of monks sinks to only 7.5% of all males. The percentage of families in this county researched that had a son or daughter in a monastery was far under the number usually given in this context.[16]

Other Lines of Business

Trade was the most significant line of business outside that of agriculture. Its importance for all the social categories of the whole county is not to be underestimated. Income received through trade could not be audited by the government or private landlord and so was not taxed. The subject could escape the confines of his village on the long trade journeys (Aziz 1978, 100f); besides this, trade and profit making was generally highly esteemed (Aziz 1969, 158). Every subject of all three categories could leave on a business trip providing that he had someone to take his place at home and carry out his duties during his leave of absence. There was no organised trade in the county. The agricultural products of the county could only be sold in markets no further than a three day trek away from the village. The county had no market place of it own. Such markets only existed in cities that housed district administrations.

Wandering tradesmen satisfied the need for consumer goods. These men carried their wares packed on donkeys or mules and regularly visited the individual counties. The trader tried to provide a broad range of goods, but food was primarily sold: sugar, rice, flour and various sorts of tea. Animal traders also wandered through the countryside, doing their business in villages. In the last years of Tibetan independence, traders from Phag-ri had rented a house in the county to serve as a trade depot which much improved the provision of consumer goods. This small business needed no license and was not taxed.

Some of the farmers also practised a handicraft in addition to their farmwork. There were no craftsmen in the county who carried out their craft to the exclusion of farmwork. The blacksmiths were despised; they were a closed society that passed the trade knowledge down from father to son. An outsider could find no admittance to the group and because of the disdain most people had for them, not very many would have wanted to. Among the blacksmiths themselves, the formation of groups was more obvious than among other craftsmen (Rauber-Schweizer 1976, 93ff). There were no resident blacksmiths in the county investigated. Families of blacksmiths would wander throughout the land setting up their tents in a village only long enough to finish the work needed there and then moving on. There was, however, a carpenter living in the village of monastic subjects and a silversmith in the village of the governmental tax-payers with whom I could speak. It was said also that tailors and masons had lived in the county previously.

Those craftsmen who practised the same craft were bound together in a sort of guild, as already discussed under the chapter on group building. The guilds were based on the district cities, where annual assemblies were held. The chairman of the guild announced to the craftsmen the extent and manner of taxes and services that would be required of them by the government for the coming year. The craftsmen of each individual guild in the district had to delegate one of their members to carry out the tax services for one year. Each of the others then paid this delegate six to seven *rdo tshad*. This tax system of the craftsmen was somewhat similar to the 'military tax" in this respect. It was the general rule that each craftsman had to work for the government one year in his life. Besides this service tax there was no further taxation of the income of the craftsmen.

These artisans only worked under commission and often directly in the home of the customer, who offered him room and board for the length of time it took him to finish the project. Three *srang* or 1/4 *khal* of grain per day was the earlier wage for a carpenter, later he received six to seven *srang* and sometimes up to ten *srang*. Goldsmiths and artists were better paid and they often received a gift of butter or a piece of meat in addition to their wages.

The learning of a craft - with the exception of that of the blacksmith - was theoretically open to all people, but it was usually the case that the son learned it from his father. If a subject of the noble or monastic estate desired to learn a trade by a master in a different category, then he had to have the permission of his landlord before moving into the house of his teacher. There he was housed and fed but not given any wages. Compared to agriculture, crafts played only a minor role in the social and economic life of the county.

Hunting could have appeared as a way of earning one's living along with that of trade and handicrafts but it was forbidden on principle by the government (Cassinelli/Ekvall 1969, 261). This law was annually redeclared in a circular sent out to all villages, but some people hunted anyway. The hunt was a chase with dogs. There were no ceremonies as, for instance, hunting magic. When a person was caught breaking the law by the village headman, he was warned to not hunt in the future as it could ruin the reputation of the whole county and lead to reprisals and punishments.

The Division of Agricultural Labour

The extensive social and economic equality found between women and men also prevented there being a sharp division between the kind of work the two had to do. The following rules were those that occurred in most relationships; they could, however, be dropped or changed at any time: It was a general rule that men did the outdoor work and that the women were responsible for all work within the home. Seed was sown by both men and women together, but ploughing and harrowing was usually considered men's work. The women watered the fields and milked the cows; children and youths tended the animals, and grain was threshed and winnowed by both men and women. When the husband practised a craft, then the woman fulfilled all the agricultural tasks.

Foodstuffs and Essential Goods

Tsampa (*rtsam pa*) was the staple food; it was barley flour prepared in a special manner; the kernels were first washed with water, then roasted with hot sand and ground to flour. This flour was then mixed with dried cheese, butter, and tea to a stiff dough. This, when shaped into small balls, was the cereal that was eaten with meat or tea. In this part of Tibet, rice and wheat flour was imported from India or Bhutan. These expensive foods were only eaten on holidays and special occasions. The bread or yeast doughs that had been so popular in East Tibet were not eaten in the county under research. In addition to Tsampa, butter and meat (sheep and yak flesh - sometimes goat) were also used as protein. There was only a very limited choice of vegetables, mainly radishes and potatoes, which were added with meat to a soup. Buttered and salted tea and *chang*, an alcoholic brew similar to beer that was made at home by every housewife, were the main beverages.

Material was woven by the women themselves whenever possible, otherwise a male weaver would come into the home and finish the cloth. Everyday-clothes were also sewn at home; the tailor was hired to make special outfits. Most consumer goods were manufactured by the craftsmen; luxury items and imported goods from the West that were sold in Gyantse and Lha-sa did not find their way into this rural county.

Property and Power

Large amounts of landed property was a distinct sign of wealth, security and prestige (Bolte et al. 1968, 53) in the eyes of the rural population of Tibet. The nobleman, who had a good amount of the county's farmland and pasturage in his possession, enjoyed great prestige. Since the aristocratic family was only represented in the county by one of the brothers, he carried all the power and respect due to the whole family. The collective ownership of land, as in the case of the monastic estate, resulted in all members sharing the prestige which automatically meant a decrease in individuals' power in proportion to the increase in numbers. This was clearly observable in the manner in which the tenants spoke of their former landlords; the subjects of the nobility always spoke with great respect of their landlords, often only willing to report their life stories with his express permission. The large scale farmers were the only ones to criticise the noble estate in any way; their secure financial basis made it possible to hold a higher opinion of themselves. The behaviour of the tenants towards the monastic estate was to a great extent unemotional, objective and practical; the submissive demeanour worn by subjects of the nobility was strange to them. When the monastery was abolished by the Chinese, the institution of the monastic landlord was also dissolved. While on the other hand with regard to the noble estate the institution lived on for the subjects in the person of the noble landlord himself. One was friendly and benevolent towards the monks who were bearers of the Buddhist religion but the administration of the monastery was viewed sceptically. The behaviour of the governmental tax-payers was characterized by self-confidence and being used to carrying responsibilities. They, whose landlord was actually the government itself in far off Lha-sa, enjoyed the most prestige in the county after the private landlords of the other two social categories. Extensive land and the power of determination over the collective land in the county was the basis of their high social rank. This was reflected in their outward appearance which was similar to that of the stewards of the noble monastic estate; similar also was their self-confident attitude.

The governmental tax-payers were considered by all in the county to be rich and powerful; one may say that they made up the upper class. The managers of the estates and the dual-tariffed tax-payers followed, along with the large scale tenants of the private landlords who can all be considered the middle class. The tenants under them made up the upper lower class. The hired workers belonged to the lowest class. This social structure which I set up after discussing the data of social life earlier in this book is also valid for economic distinctions.

As in other cultures (Bolte et al. 1968, 75) typical differences between the judgements of strangers and that of individuals concerning social position were apparent: right down to the thin layer of hired workers, everyone classified himself as being "middle-class" when asked about his economic situation. The assessments of strangers included much finer differentiation: the governmental tax-payers were reputed by the others to be rich; they themselves considered the estate stewards and dual-tariffed tax-payers to be "middle class", the large estate tenants to be "common" and the small farmers and hired men to be "poor". The estate stewards, large scale tenants and dual-tariffed farmers considered themselves "middle class", the small farmers "common" and the hired men "poor". The small tenant farmers held the estate stewards, large scale tenants and dual-tariffed tax-payers to be "rich" along with the governmental tax-payers; themselves they thought to be "middle class" and the hired men were "poor". The hired men, however, also considered the small tenant farmers to be "poor" along with themselves; all others were "rich".

As far as our knowledge reaches, one may say that a subject of a particular landlord stood in a binding dependency to him. The influence of a landlord over his subjects was, however, limited by certain factors. The lack of labourers is to be mentioned here in the first place (Aziz 1969, 187). Many subjects of the nobility stressed the fact that a landlord was often willing to make many concessions to a subject in order to keep a hard working and reliable steward. The dependent relationship could not usually be legally terminated but anyone could secretly run away. Besides this economic factor, the landlord, who needed hardworking tenants in order to yield a high enough profit, was also pressured by social factors. An example will elucidate this: once when the noble landlord had slapped his young steward, his prestige had immediately dropped; in order to "save face" he had had to compensate the steward to a certain extent. If a landlord wanted to be respected and his position demanded it, he had to show himself bound to the Buddhist norms of compassion, benevolence and generosity. An open infringement of these norms was always accompanied by a "loss of face". The higher the social rank of the person, the less he could afford such a loss. Then there was also the possibility of a type of civil disobedience, which, though not practised by the inhabitants of the county researched, did in effect limit the landlords' arbitrariness. Such civil strife is reported from the estates of the Sa-skya (Casinelli/Ekvall 1969, 344f).

The economic system of Tibet was based upon the liability of the subjects to pay taxes of natural goods and manual labour. These taxes were levied by the state by binding the subject to a landlord or placing him under the jurisdiction of the nearest district governor. Supported by a certain bureacratic administration this system almost guaranteed that the farmer would remain on his land and through his cultivation of it, provide a steady flow of natural goods. Coercion, that is so often based upon an economic system (Johnson 1960, 205f) was practised by the government in that the subject's freedom of movement was limited; the leasing of tenant land and the establishment of a modest but adequate standard of living was so successful as to make the subjects unwilling to leave the system. Coercion was brought to bear above all in the transmitting of the social value system. The established, land owning farmer felt himself to be a respected member of the community; the landless tramp was a despised "drop-out". This coercion held the economic situation in Tibet stable for many hundreds of years.

The ruling economic system was not suited to maximizing profits, the usual yield was much more often looked upon as being the norm. Almost half the profits of the noble and monastic estates were returned to the subjects in the form of provisions and salaries, and the governmental tax-payers delivered a relatively large proportion of their annual income to the state as taxes. This had the effect of preventing large amounts of wealth from being hoarded by the extensively landed gentry, and on the other hand assured that a certain amount of the total proceeds flowed into the poorer social levels by way of remuneration. It contributed to the prevention of sharp divisions being formed between the rich and the poor; this balancing tendency in the Tibetan economic system was a further factor in the stability of the social structure.

VIII. THE POLITICAL STRUCTURE OF THE COUNTY

The political structures of rural communities have been investigated often enough (Carrasco 1959, 133ff; Aziz 1978, 186ff) so that here only the information directly related to the three communities of the county researched will be reported. The counties were delighted with their extensive amount of autonomy. The authorities, i.e. the district governor, noble landlord, etc., very seldom came to the county. They could only interfere with the inner administration of the county when not enough taxes were being paid. Although taxation rates had at one time been set by the landlord, he could neither arbitrarily raise the rates, nor have his own people collect the taxes personally. There was no police station or military post in the county. Only with the express permission of the village headman could soldiers be sent there, except of course in time of war.

Each of the three categories of subjects which respectively peopled one of the three villages, had its "speaker". This person was one of the farmers and represented their interests to the landlord; on the other hand, the "speaker" also had to relay the requests of the landlord to the community. It has already often been pointed out in this book that this institution is dysfunctional in the strict sense of the reason of State, but that it also damped social unrest so that the system was able to stay constant for hundreds of years.

The position of "speaker" for the category of governmental tax-payers involved the most power, for he was also the village headman (*rgan po*). He was elected by all the governmental tax-payers. Sometimes the oracle played as big a role in these elections as custom and tradition (only members of certain families were eligible). If, for instance, they were not able to agree on a person, or did not want to take the responsibility for choosing one, then they often left the choice to the oracle. The village headman was usually re-elected every year, yet in the county under investigation the village headman had been in office for several decades since everyone was apparently satisfied with him.

The duties of the village headman were not very extensive. The most important and respected duty was the delivery of tax tributes to the district governor (*rdzong dpon*). From his direct contact with the district administration, the village headman also received authority to arbitrate over small conflicts in the village and give out advice. His function in the village then, was to smooth and channelize negative emotions and help prevent the breaking of laws. The extent of his influence was directly related to the strength and popularity of his character. He could only make decisions in consultation with the rest of the governmental tax-payers. Whenever the county as a whole came in contact with the authorities, then the village headman also represented the other two categories of subjects.

Should the village headman misuse his office, by favouring relatives for instance, then the community of governmental tax-payers was free to depose him and elect another. This action needed the approval of the district administration. The village headman had neither judicial authority nor did he function as a policeman; these jobs were reserved for the district governor. Nor had he any insignia or other signs of his post.

A second official stood at the village headman's side; he was called *rgan chung*, literally, "small village elder". His duty was to organize the governmental transports and the construction of bridges and roads.

One should probably rather speak of a collective leadership by the whole community of governmental tax-payers because the leading role of the village headman was rather weak. Collective dependency and taxation demanded collective authority.

The speakers for the two other categories of subjects were chosen from the respective groups of tenants by the landlords, and named estate-stewards. Their function was limited to easing tensions and promoting good will. In relation to their own groups, the position of steward was not so different from that of the village headman yet, in regard to the authorities above them, there was a substantial difference. The landlord could demote the steward at any time, furthermore he had a *phyag mdzod* placed over him. The steward could at most appeal to his landlord, but not to the district governor who held a higher position then the private landlord.

Judicial authority was in the hands of the district governor alone. If a criminal was to be arrested, then a group of villagers lead by the headman pursued him to deliver him up to the district administration. The county was fairly helpless against an attack by bands of thieves, as soldiers had to be sent from far off Gyantse. Apart from murder or manslaughter the villagers considered criminal acts done within the boundaries of the county to be their own affair and they were settled internally. Naturally then the sentences would be somewhat milder here than before the district court. The reputation of a family was sometimes of great importance to the outcome of a trial in the county. Since members of the same "we-group" invariably would be called upon at one time or another to pass judgement on each other, it was highly advisable from each individual's point of view to preserve at least the appearance of social peace within the group.

In summary: The county had no possibility of influencing the decisions of the superior district administration. The only requirement worth mentioning for the county was to deliver its taxes and to do its obligatory labour for the state. Excepting these responsibilities, the county was relatively autonomous and could allow small crimes to pass unnoticed by the official judicary system. The leadership of the county was in the hands of the governmental tax-payers, who for their part, elected a village headman and his representative. His authority was limited and he could only use it in concurrence with the rest of his group.

IX. CHANGES MADE IN THE TRADITIONAL SOCIAL STRUCTURES OF TIBET BY THE PEOPLE'S REPUBLIC OF CHINA

The Sources

There is probably no other third world country that has astounded the world's public as much as the People's Republic of China. Some call it a rigid system for creating universal equality; others see in it a creative concept full of possibilities for the development of the third world countries. The removal of the bitterest consequences of poverty, corruption and economic failure, as well as the upheavals involved in the cultural revolution caused the world to pay attention, confused people's opinions and led to contrasting judgments depending on the observer's own particular political convictions.

Surveying the living conditions of the various minorities that live in the People's Republic today, and make up a considerable portion of the population, a dazzling economic advancement has undeniably taken place and can be verified by ample statistical material. The question remains open, however, how much of a share the normal man has in this. Parallels with the Third Reich force themselves upon us, but I do not want to go further into that. The momentary phase of liberalization and apparent humanisation under Deng Hsiao-ping is still too recent to be correctly evaluated. The Democracy Wall, first established and soon afterwards removed, shows how unstable the situation has become.

The available information on minorities is completely different from that concerning the dominant group of — the modern term is "Han" — true Chinese. We find ourselves confronted with arguments full of contradictory opinions whereby each claims alone to represent the truth. The events, overwhelming, brutal and impressive, demand a personal response that even the scholar cannot avoid if he does not want to stop at the parroting of statistically documented information. My personal opinions will be clearly expressed at the end of this chapter, but first of all, it is necessary to explain the sources of information that are available today by which the Chinese government in Tibet can be evaluated.

One can classify the information at hand according to its particular relationship to certain events. Yet one always comes up against the same contradictions that spring from the attitudes of the various authors. It would be preferable to sort the information in terms of the conviction of the authors and the way they handle the sources.

1. The publications of the People's Republic of China should be mentioned first. In the magazines *Peking Review*, *China Reconstructs* and others, several articles about Tibet have appeared, each of which portrayed a socialistic idyll of flag flying children, radiant and brave young men, etc. The verification of these reports, however, is impossible. The same is true of such publications as *Tibet Today*.[1]

More information can be found in the Chinese and Communist Tibetan press. In the press releases and official statements one can, with experience and dexterity, uncover hints as to actual events, and can see through the veil of socialist hymns. Unfortunately these sources are available to Western scholars only in a very limited way. One is then all the more thankful for the collection of Chinese magazine articles about Tibet put together by the Union Research Institute in the volume *Tibet 1950 - 1967*. The programme of Radio Lha-sa also belong to this category, however one only receives this information indirectly, through the Tibetan refugee press in India.

2. Related to the propaganda magazines of the People's Republic are reports of some westerners who were authorized, mostly by Mao Tse-tung himself, to travel through Tibet.[2] Because all these people had close links with the Chinese Communist Party and its former leader they were able to obtain entry visas

for Tibet, which was then out of the reach of anybody else. None of these visitors to Tibet had any knowledge of Tibetan history and civilization. In their reports they wrote down exactly what their Chinese informants told them. For this reason these records reflect the Chinese image of Tibetans and Tibetan culture but not the actual state of modern Tibet. Sometimes these publications amuse the Tibetologist, when, for example, he is told that the doctrine of institutional reincarnation was established during the reign of the Fifth Dalai Lama (17th century), who - according to Han Suyin (1977, 16), - was the first to bear the title Dalai Lama. The historical truth is that this Mongolian title was given to the Third Dalai Lama and that the doctrine of reincarnation was set up during the early 13th century. These books and articles in general contribute to our psychological knowledge but not to our information on communist Tibet.

3. The propaganda used to justify the encroachment of the Chinese is vigorously opposed by the public organs of the Tibetan refugees in the West and in India. Numerous reports from refugees, also from those who left Tibet in the last years, are published in magazines like *Bod-mi-rang-dbang* and *Tibetan Review*. They are marked by personal sufferings and sometimes show those deficiencies that are typical of people not used to portraying events in an exact and detailed manner. Generalized complaints against the Chinese are accumulated in these reports without revealing what exactly took place. However, I know from years of experience with Tibetans that this is not necessarily a sign of untrustworthiness but rather of modesty.

The organizations for exiled Tibetans have recently begun to recognize this lack of precision and are trying to document exactly the sufferings of the Tibetan people.[3] Two works especially should be mentioned here: *Tibet under Chinese Communist Rule* and *Tibet, the Undying Flame*, the latter written by Kunzang Paljor in the Tibetan language. The first book contains twenty-seven cases in which the individual Tibetans are identified exactly by name, place of birth, profession etc., and then their personal stories follow, describing what they experienced and why they fled to India. These eye-witness reports can reveal the truth to the observant reader. The second book gives a broad review of the economic, social and cultural changes that took place from 1950 to 1969. In this, the economic progress that was to an extent achieved is not neglected. The author is a very talented young man, raised and educated by the Chinese, who worked for years as the chief editor of the Lha-sa daily paper and thereby was exposed to an extraordinarily large amount of information. The book was translated into English, but this edition was unfortunately not at my disposal.

Europeans and Americans who lived in Tibet during the critical years from 1948 to 1959 also wrote down their experiences (Moraes 1960; Ford 1957). These are useful sources because they were usually familiar with Tibetan life before the Chinese came and so were able to compare it with later conditions. The personal experiences of the individuals prevail in these reports. Being free from Utopian ideologies, valuable information is found in them.

In a certain sense the many autobiographies written by Tibetans are similar to the reports from Europeans. They try to make a small nation's tragedy tangible through the prism of an individual's fate.[4] It is understandable in this situation that some of the unpleasantness of the past loses its definition and that the present sufferings under the Chinese are more in focus. Nevertheless one is surprised to find no bitterness or hate towards the Chinese. The majority of the religious Tibetans who had to leave all their worldly possessions in their homeland, give a religious interpretation to their fate as refugees, seeing it as a chance to free themselves from or to reduce their entanglement in worldly covetousness (Dawa Norbu 1974, 198f). They perceive it to be their *karma* which cannot be escaped through hate or aggression but only by a moral life and religious devotion.

4. Only a very limited number of publications have evaluated these sources and tried to give a verifiable picture of the events since 1959.[5] Since primary sources in the form of archive material, field research, etc., are not yet available, most investigators are waiting for an improvement in research

facilities. Journalists have recently made many attempts to illuminate and evaluate the situation in communist Tibet. Some however lack a fundamental knowledge of pre-Chinese Tibet so they run the risk of misunderstanding the present situation, though most western journalists try to render a well-balanced report.

Peter Aufschnaiter, who together with Heinrich Harrer escaped from a British Indian concentration camp into Tibet during the second world war, received permission in 1972 to revisit Tibet. He related his experiences to me in 1973 during his visit to Munich, a year before his death. His narrative was very depressing; he, for the most part, agreed with those descriptions given by the Tibetan refugees. Aufschnaiter seemed to me to be a reliable witness because he had mastered the Tibetan language and could really communicate with the native Tibetans; he was familiar with old Tibet through many years of residence; and - this I found especially important - was not dominated by any particular ideology.

It is not my purpose here to give a complete bibliographic review of the publications concerned with Tibet, but only to give certain criteria by which the various publications can be evaluated.

To follow, I will use a case study to show what has changed in the social and economic structure of the farming county, what results this has had on the lives of people and under what kinds of political conditions they were living.

Phases of the Chinese Assumption of Power

Before turning to the actual changes that have occurred, the individual phases of the Chinese path to power must be mentioned. China found, by recourse to historical events many centuries ago and which are still contested as to their power of testimony, an arbitrary reason for military operations which began on the East Tibetan border in Amdo and Khams and finally expanded to include the entire country. For one familiar with historical Tibetan literature, there is no question as to the fact that this "justification" is based upon historical falsification, a method employed especially by totalitarian states to rationalize their territorial expansion.

In 1949 the People's Republic of China began a propaganda battle, announcing that Tibet had been forced by American and English imperialists to declare itself independent in 1912, while actually the imperialists planned to exploit the Tibetan people and their economic resources. The duty of the Tibetan government was, therefore, to fight against these imperialists and the Chinese declared themselves prepared to help the Tibetans. In these propaganda speeches, the inner autonomy of Tibet, especially as regarding religion and traditions was always assured.[6] Since neither the Tibetan government nor the people responded to this call, the Chinese army crossed the Tibetan border in the Khams province on the seventh of October, 1950, and began therewith the battle for the subjugation of Tibet that is probably not finished even today (Peissel 1973, 67ff; Andrugstsang 1973, 55ff). For a long time this war did not lead to any clear determination of power. China was able to achieve several military successes in open battle because of her relatively modern weapons - aircraft and bombings played their part - yet the Tibetans in their fight for freedom exploited the natural impassability of the land and developed their own sort of guerilla strategy (Peissel 1973, 103ff).

Wherever the Chinese had been able to take military control, they introduced reforms as far as they felt they could, considering the unstable political balance. One cannot therefore cite a particular date from which the Red Chinese began reforming Tibet; neither can one assume that the changes were simultaneously or commensurately inaugurated all over Tibet. They were set in motion at various places with different degrees of intensity and continuity. The pressure to revise socio-economic structures to resemble the Chinese models was always present. Success or failure was dependent upon the changing concepts of authority.

In general the following phases can be distinguished. Between 1950 and 1954 the Chinese limited themselves to winning the ruling classes of Tibet to their side. Tours of China for nobles and religious leaders were financed; the nobles were admitted to the newly formed Revolutionary Committee and decorated with honours and new offices; monasteries were restored; the Communist Party of China (CCP) also offered the traditional alms to the monks – for instance during the sMon-lam festival in Lhasa. Politically the Chinese sought to promote factionalism in that they set up the central government of the Dalai Lama as a rival to the Pan-chen Lama and as being opposed to the east Tibetan Chamdo region. This increased the existing disunity and weakness of the Tibetan situation (Ginsburgs/Mathos 1967, 40; Andrutsang 1973, 69ff). Structural changes in society and the economy had not yet been accomplished at this time, but probably had been planned and in part introduced.

The villages of the region under research lay in the central government region of Tibet. Contact between its inhabitants and the Chinese was superficial and life still passed according to the traditional pattern of Tibet. However, the relationship between the Tibetan government and officials on the one side, and the CCP and the Chinese People's Liberation Army on the other side, was strained from the very beginning and small conflicts often broke out (Ginsburgs/Mathos 1964, 49ff).

The "Preparatory Committee for the Autonomous Region of Tibet" was introduced in 1955, (Tibet 1968, 140ff). The Chinese had cleverly so mixed-up the Tibetan government with the organs of the CCP, that, to outside observers, Tibet was truly a part of the multinational state of China. Now the CCP and the People's Liberation Army (PLA) had a better chance of applying pressure to the Tibetan administration so that they would take up the path of socialism. If the Chinese had up to 1955 at least verbally restricted all adverse criticism of the religion and its practioners, it now distorted the foundations of the Tibetan system in such a manner, that communist assertions about the "feudal slave regime" were apparently justified. A good example of this change in political climate was the article written as a "letter to the editor" about the "counter-revolutionary intrigues" of the monks in the Tibetan region Kannan (Tibet 1968, 248ff no 50). The fact that a few monasteries possessed land labourers and tenants is presented here as if the monasteries wilfully exploited the rural population. During the years from 1955 - 59 the communists also attacked the institutions of the county. The incidents of brutal attacks by Chinese soldiers on the civilian population increased; people were arrested; children were forced into Chinese schools or were deported to China; the village headmen were deposed, accused of various crimes by a hired or blackmailed "witness", and sent to a forced labour camp. Yet for the large majority of the population, life followed, to a certain extent, its usual course, even if the "new times" announced themselves here and there in unimaginable, upsetting events (Dawa Norbu 1974, 102ff).

The Tibetan/Chinese war in the eastern regions of Tibet (Peissel 1973, 135ff; Andrutsang 1973, 65ff), the expansion of Chinese military bases in central and western Tibet, with the increasing oppression of the civilian population;[7] the degradation of the Tibetan culture;[8] the reprisals undertaken against monasteries, temples and religious communities (International Commission of Jurists 1960, 14ff), leads finally to the March revolution of 1959, in the confusion of which the Dalai Lama fled to India. He was followed by the exodus of a considerable portion of the Tibetan people. The total population was probably about six million people (Shakabpa 1967, 6); about 3 - 4 million had lived in the two central provinces of dBus and gTsang (Richardson 1962, 6). A further 2.7 million had settled in other provinces of Tibet (Tibet 1968, 78). About 80,000 Tibetans fled to the countries bordering Tibet on the south; the large majority of these refugees come from the two central provinces so that almost 2.5% of the residents of central Tibet chose the distress of flight and all the worries of life as an emigrant over life under the communist rule. In order to stop this mass flight, the Chinese ordered the temporary suspension of all agricultural and mercantile taxes and compulsory labour.[9] The prospect of an economic system free from taxes or labour duty motivated many Tibetan farmers to work especially hard and forget the foreign domination. The years from 1959 - 62 can be called a period of reconciliation. In 1963 the revolutionary committees were reorganized in order to supervise the transformation of all aspects of Tibetan life. The benefits of 1959 were recalled. The expropriation of the broad masses was now systematically undertaken whereas the ruling classes, and those Tibetans who had been involved in the resistance movements, had already had their possessions expropriated in 1959. The social and economic institutes of the land were transformed according to Chinese communist maxims.

The Cultural Revolution in Tibet from 1966 - 69 was a heavy blow to the country. The Tibetans watched with astonishment the struggle between rival groups of Chinese. The destruction of monasteries and temples hit them the hardest, first of all the Jo-khang in Lha-sa, the famous temple that had been built in the seventh century AD. by King Srong-btsan-sgam-po.[10] The Jo-khang was the chief Buddhist edifice in Tibet, comparable to St. Peter's in Rome or Solomon's Temple in Jerusalem. The goal of the Cultural Revolution was the annihilation of the "four elders": the old ideology, the old culture, the old traditions and the old habits (Tibet 1968, 600). It is obvious that people who had already suffered under the forced changes, should feel the collapse of the cultural system especially hard to bear. The continuity of their socio-cultural identity was so threatened that many Tibetans felt that the only outlet was the now much more dangerous flight across the Himalayan mountains, or suicide. In spite of the heavily guarded mountain passes, small groups of refugees were again and again able to escape to India or Nepal. A few armed groups of freedom fighters from Amdo and Khams were able to fight their whole way diagonally across Tibet and arrive in India in 1972.

An increasing liberalization has been observed since 1970. The Tibetans were allowed to wear their national costumes again, Tibetan holidays might be celebrated as such; in some places it seems as if a re-establishment of religious life had been allowed (Tibetan Review VIII no 5, 4). The liberalizing tendency was viewed as being so profound as to lead some to believe that the Red-Chinese would be ready for a political reversal. There were rumours of secret negotiations between the Dalai Lama and the Chinese government and of a return of Tibetans to their homeland in the near future (Patterson 1973, 29f).

Since Mao Tse-tung's death, the deposing of the "gang of four", and above all since the government of Deng Hsiao-ping 37 Tibetans have been released from the Lha-sa prison. They were also promised permission to leave Tibet for India if they wished (Tibetan Review XIII, 11, 5; and XIII, 12, 5). Tibetan delegations and dance groups visited Asiatic and European lands, where they also were allowed to contact Tibetans living in exile (Tibetan Review XIII, 12, 7f). During 1979 some Tibetan refugees managed to visit their relatives in Tibet and a few of them gave their impressions in the magazine Tibetan Review (XIV, 5, p.6f; XV, 1, p.4). An official delegation, headed by Lobsang Samten, the Dalai Lama's younger brother, toured for three months through Tibet. The officials tried to find the facts about the apparent change in the Chinese attitude towards the Tibetans (Tibetan Review XIV, 8, p. 7f and XV, 1, p.6). From Indian newspapers, I learnt that a second tour of this delegation is scheduled to continue the negotiations with the Chinese authorities, though the outcomes of the talks are still unpredictable. If the Chinese government really concede a kind of inner autonomy, cultural as well religious, to the Tibetans, the Tibetan issue may become settled. This would indeed be evidence of the humanization of the communist ideology in China.

The Changing Milieu

Technical advances in large areas of Tibet, including the Gyantse district, directly affected the farming population. The old caravan highways leading out from Gyantse were expanded and improved so that they were passable for the heavy military convoys (Tibet 1968, 135f; Chen 1965, 24ff; Karan 1976, 47). As earlier, the roads had to be built by the people who lived along them, only Tibetan workers were now given their orders by the Chinese military.[11] Gyantse received an airport that also was built by Tibetans.

Labour groups were successfully recruited by the Chinese using the old Tibetan method. The Chinese requested that the local Tibetan administration put a certain number of workers at their disposal. The Tibetan administrations then turned to the new village headman to whom the unpleasant task fell of finding people for this compulsory work (*'u lag*). When not enough local residents volunteered then the quota was filled with beggars and orphans (Dawa Norbu 1974, III). This case from the Sa-sKya region has exemplary significance: whenever the Tibetan system seemed useful for the Red-Chinese they took advantage of it, ignoring the fact that it was otherwise called slavery.

The improved transport systems and roads were thought of as military corridors in case of war and during peace they were to help the transport of military goods and to control the entire land. In the 1960's, only military vehicles and the automobiles of the party organization could use these roads. If a Tibetan had wanted to visit someone in the next county, then the application, justification and examination for the trip took much more time than it had earlier taken to complete the journey by foot or donkey. A Tibetan was seldom allowed to make a trip of over 20 or 30 miles. Visiting relatives was usually not considered a sufficient enough cause for such permission. The time taken over the trip had to be made up by working over-time before and after the actual journey. Similar stipulations were connected with the mail and telegraph services; for a long time all use of such equipment was reserved for the Chinese, but now the whole situation is involved in a radical change.

The village changed little in its basic structure. Those families who had owned cottages could remain there, while those with larger or better furnished homes had to turn them over without compensation to the rulers for use as meeting places, office buildings, etc.. This testimony of the Tibetans agreed completely with that of P. Aufschnaiter, who reported that the outward appearance of Tibetan villages in the area of Lake Manasarova had not changed much at all in the last 30 years, ignoring the fact that there are hardly any religious monuments or buildings left today.

What was earlier a county (*brgya tsho*) is now called *gzhi kha*. Its attachment to a district capital (*rdzong*) remained under the same circumstances. The researched hundred-county, however, was reallocated in 1959 to a *rdzong* that had been named a district capital by the Chinese administration in 1960; before that it had been just another hundred-county similar to the one researched and had had the same status. The new county (*gzhi kha*) had an administrative centre, a police station and a small public health office. Next to this was the county meeting place. There were no shops in the county, these were only found in the district cities (*rdzong*). Since the families were no longer as large as they used to be, because of deportations and forced resettlement, one house usually held more than one family. However, since these homes were not rebuilt as multiple-family apartments, and several families had to share one kitchen, it gave every opportunity for quarrels, mutual distrust and discord.

The provision of household water stayed the same. Fuel, usually yak dung, was no longer allowed to be bought or sold. Apparently the dung was used to fertilize the fields and its use as fuel was reduced by only allowing yak dung that was gathered personally to be burned.

The villages have lost their character as specific settlements of individual categories of subjects, since these abolished in the years after 1959. The population of the villages and counties have experienced a basic transformation. Earlier one could observe that most of the inhabitants had lived in a single locality for generations; today just the opposite is true: parts of county communities were resettled hundreds of miles away from their original homes. Refugees that have been able to flee in the last few years have all reported that there are often only three or four of the old village families left in the new communities.

The primary groups of these villages have been severely damaged by the relocation of communities. The former familiarity, the "neighbourliness" and recognition, that gave confidence to the individual as well as social position made way for a general distrust and a large amount of insecurity. My observations have shown that this destruction of village primary groups is a factor that has struck Tibetans a much harder blow than other more obvious difficulties. Robbed of his village primary group and his extended family, the Tibetan today finds himself for the first time in his history face to face with a world whose actions he can only perceive in terms of unjustifiable use of violence. Chinese authorities planned and pursued this social isolation in order to make the Tibetans more open for communist indoctrination. Similar methods could be observed in the Korean war, used against American prisoners of war (Mann 1972, 25ff and 36ff). Fear of social isolation often caused the Tibetans to leave their country as refugees; this could be observed especially among the hired shepherds and sharecroppers. The particular consistency of neighbourhood and primary groups induced numerous tenants, hired men, and settlers to follow their former landlord into exile.

The New Social Life

When, after 1959, the Dalai Lama and his cabinet (*bka shag*) no longer even nominally constituted the head of the Tibetan state, the Pan-chen Lama occupied this position for a while[12] until he had to abdicate in the confusion of the Cultural Revolution (Tibet 1968, 700). The government was slowly infiltrated according to the Chinese plan and dissolved piece by piece. Under the watchful eye of the Committee for the Autonomous Region of Tibet, which was to a large extent conceived of and run by the Chinese, district committees were established. Ginsburg and Mathos (1964, 111) arrived at the conclusion that the "fact that this whole scheme, if successful, would spell the death of the former structure of Tibetan government, leaving it a shrunken head without a body". Under the pretext of there not being any qualified Tibetans available, all the key positions were filled with Chinese. The resident Tibetan population were under-represented in various political committees and unions for many more years; of the fifty-six members of the Committee for the Autonomous Region of Tibet, only three were Tibetans in August, 1971, when the new chairman was to be elected. Two of the three Tibetans had Chinese names; all three were secretaries. On the lower level of the executive branch the picture was the same: when, in June 1972, three communist party committees at the level below the region and one at the city level had to be formed, there were only six Tibetans among the 293 delegates. Even the city committee in Lha-sa, that is often thought of as being a show piece for outsiders, and which consists of thirty-nine committee members, eight rotating members, eight secretaries and nineteen permanent representatives, only had two Tibetans among them, both of whom were secretaries. In the past few years this ratio has improved a little to the benefit of the Tibetans. In 1977 there were six Tibetans posted among the fifteen committee members of the standing committee of the Tibet Autonomous Region. Only one of the Tibetan delegates, Mrs. Pasang, actually came from Tibet, all the others had joined the Chinese communists during the time of the "long march", before the communists in China had come to power (Tibetan Review VIII no 5, 4 and XIII no 11, 5; Karan 1976, 33).

Military and party administrations were also in Chinese hands (Tibet 1968, 520). Only very few Tibetans - like the Pan-chen Lama, Nga-bo, and some others who also usually came from the noble classes - were put in top positions.

The typical characteristics of Tibetan administration, namely that the ruling institutions were represented by people who belonged to the "we-group" of the ruled and that authority was delegated to several people to avoid a direct show of force by the government - these characteristics were gradually weakened from 1955 - 1959 and were lost in 1959. From then on Tibet was ruled by foreigners who were not bound to the subjects in any way, neither through culture, language, religion or tradition. The rulers' ideology and interests were fundamentally different from those of the people. The new rulers asserted their claim to power with the help of the army.[13]

The three categories of subjects that had existed in Tibet since long ago were, for the most part, disbanded in 1959. A few monastic estates that stood under the protection of the Pan-chen Lama were tolerated for a few more years before they too were expropriated. With the suspension of the subject categories, the entire economic structure collapsed and essential regulations for social life could no longer stand. In the socio-economic vacuum that arose afterwards, the communist rulers presented their ordinances to make Tibet a part of China and at the same time get the most economic use out of the country.

The Tibetan people are divided today into seven levels according to the profession they practise or the area they live in (Kunsang Paljor 1971, 1): 1. farmers, 2. nomads, 3. traders, 4. city-folk, 5. Tibetan cadres, 6. those attending elementary school, and 7. those attending intermediate school. Through these levels there runs a kind of class system that evaluates the individual according to his former social category as compared to communist ideology: 1. the rulers (*mnga' bdag*), 2. the representatives of the rulers, 3. the wealthy, 4. the middle class, 5. the poor and 6. the counter-revolutionaries (*log spyod*) (op. cit. p.2; Dhondup Choedon 1978, 32ff). The first three classes and the sixth class were declared the enemies of the people. All their possessions were confiscated without compensation, delcared to be the property of the Chinese government and the profits thereof were transported to China (loc. cit; Tibet 1968, 596). Some of the members of these classes were executed, though children and youths under 18 years of age were spared. The manner in which these classifications were distributed is shown by the former village headman of the governmental tax-payers being classified as a "ruler", sent to prison, and then to a forced labour camp. The stewards of the noble and monastic estates were classified as "representatives of the rulers" and the governmental tax-payers were determined to be "wealthy". The classification of individuals has been strictly practised in all aspects of life since 1959.

· The new classes determine the future fate of those who belong to them even more strictly than the earlier subject categories. In 1959 the motto "one should cooperate with the middle-class farmers, one should support the poor" (*zhing 'bring la mthun 'brel byed/dbul phons la bstun dgos*) was given out through the Chinese authorities. In practice this meant that members of these two classes alone were considered normal citizens, all others - and this was the majority of the population - were subject to "special handling". So the children of the other four categories received only a limited education,[14] their applications for medical attention were often delayed, applications for permission to leave the village were rejected, and they were always last in the distribution of food. Yet the worst fate was the treatment called "education", (*slob sbyong*), it ranged from public slander and degradation to physical beatings and the hardest forced labour. One aspect of this "education" namely the cleaning of toilets, was experienced by all members of these four classes, not even children of six years of age were exempt (Kunsang Paljor 1971, 3).

When one compares the old subject category system with the new class system, then the following picture becomes clear: the former lower middle class (private tenants) were classified as "middle-class farmers", the sharecroppers and hired workers, along with tramps were called "poor". The government tax-payers were classified as being "wealthy" and subjected to persecution.

The formation of groups is now only possible under certain circumstances. The informal groups of workers and the political education groups prevail. Since the members of these groups are continuously replaced and exchanged, the formation of the primary groups that had been so plentiful in Tibetan social life is prevented. One of the most important new groups is the so-called "mutual-aid-team" (*rogs res tshogs pa*); 90% of all Tibetan field workers were members of it in 1964. These groups were a preparation for the introduction of communes; although the farmers still owned a part of their former land they worked on it collectively. Agricultural tools and machines that had been rented from the state, were held in common by the whole group. In many ways this group is comparable to the former tenant communities of the earlier estates.

With the dissolving of the three types of landlords, the categories of subjects dependent upon them were released from the relationship that had existed between landlord and tax-payer or tenant.

If the farmer had previously received a piece of land to cultivate deliberately in return for taxes and compulsory labour, then he now usually received a much smaller piece of land, and had to deliver half its yield to the authorities without any compensation. The amount and extent of compulsory labour have remained the same, only that now the commands are given by a stranger and the people often suffer from time deadlines and lack of adequate provision. The normal working day in a commune lasts eight hours, however in autumn it can be as long as sixteen hours (Dhondub Choedon 1978, 19). A farmer had always had the certainty that the landlord could not dismiss him, but now he does not know how long he can stay in his present situation, when the next campaign will be started or whether he might be accused of some "crime" and sent to prison. Nor does the subject have any chance of dissolving the new dependency relationship; the only possibility is to undertake the difficult flight over the Himalayan mountains into Nepal, Bhutan or India. Not even the sick or old are released from their bonds; when they can no longer do their work, they are no longer suitable propaganda tools for Communism and so receive no more food rations. A temporary suspension of this dependency is no longer possible either.

Rules that determine the dependency are set up by the Chinese according to their concept of authority, without allowing Tibetans to participate in the process. The rules change according to the political trends in the CCP and are incomprehensible to most Tibetans.

Till recent times a Tibetan might leave his village only in service of the party and state, or at least only with their permission. The former "hundred-county" continued to be divided into three villages (*grong*), between which free traffic was forbidden, at least after 1959. Lha-sa, which now has a population of about 120,000, was divided into four city districts between which pass controls had been set up; whether they still exist remains dubious. Tibetans were strictly forbidden to cross these boundaries without a written "pass". Family visits were not acceptable grounds for the issuing of such a permission - not even in cases of hardship.

Business trips for secretaries and employees of the CCP and PLA are allowed as well as prize tours for those singular Tibetans who have exceeded their work quotas by more than 150% and have always shown themselves to be true followers of Mao. Trade journeys have in general been abolished since trade was taken over by the state. A few Nepalese traders have still been allowed to travel to Lha-sa in order to import foreign wares.

One special form of local mobility was that of deportation. Adults were forced to resettle in order to open up new territories in once uninhabited areas. Families were usually not kept together during this relocation. Deportation of children has been verified in central Tibet since 1954, and sporadically in east Tibet since 1951. The International Conference of Jurists ascertained that "There is no doubt on the evidence that large numbers of children, many being tiny babies, have been taken under force or the threat of force from their homes and transferred from Tibet to China" (International Commission of Jurists 1960, 51). Children and youths were often impressed by the new regime and were willing to go to a school in China, despite the understandable protests from their families.[15]

Social mobility is now only possible through a rise or fall in the CCP. Since technology and industry have by now become somewhat established in Tibet, professions in these branches are available. The data on hand does not allow an investigation of the numbers of Tibetans who have achieved a social rise or fall through the changes that have taken place since 1959.

A few young Tibetans have been given a chance of advancement within the party. Most of them are in the offices and administration centres and officiate as go-betweens for the Chinese adminstrators and the Tibetan people. Kunsang Paljor (1971, 35ff) has revealing information regarding this. The Tibetan administrators (*las byed pa*) may be divided into three groups. The first group is very small in number; its members come from the poorest families - beggars, criminals, etc. - and stand firmly on Maoist ideology, fully representing the Chinese wishes. A very tense relationship exists between these and the rest of the Tibetans. The second group is the exact opposite; its members also come from the lower classes but they hate the Chinese as much as the first group admires them. Neither of these two groups are very well educated.

The third group, which has the most members, is made up of various classes but most of them have come from the middle class. They are critical of the old Tibetan system as practised before 1959 as well as of the new Chinese regime. They are usually well educated and study Communism intensely. This third group rejects the unequal treatment of Tibetans by the Chinese and above all protests against the violent incidents that have occurred, yet for them the Chinese are not considered enemies. One gets the impression that many Tibetans value this group highly as it seems qualified to make the transition from the old to the new acceptable to most of the Tibetan people.

All those who had formerly been in possession of a certain amount of property have had to endure a descent in social status.

The former variety in family structures was reduced to include after 1959 only monogamy. Since the Chinese administration only marriages of this kind can be entered. The polyandric and polygynic families stemming from the independent era were dissolved along with the families made up of several generations; the various parts of these families were resettled in other working areas. A newly founded family's residence is always neo-local; the political cadres of the county assign houses for each family. Large families are thereby prevented from developing. Tibetans saw therein a planned measure to keep them from becoming too prosperous. Yet, the hardest blow to the family was the party's grabbing of the Tibetan children. Deportation has already been mentioned; the school system remains to be investigated.

School Accomodation

In 1965 there were 1600 elementary schools in Tibet with 60,000 pupils (Tibet 1968, 590). The goal had been to build a school for every 100 families. P. Aufschnaiter visited such a school in 1972, that was held in a requisitioned farmhouse in western Tibet. The children memorized the works of Mao Tse-tung in Tibetan; there were no other textbooks and no other subjects. Better elementary schools were found in the central provinces and in the district capitals. Kunsang Paljor (1971, 42ff) describes the situation at the end of the 1960's: There were two types of elementary schools; one kind had been established by the government and the other by the people.

In Lha-sa there were two of the former type of schools, established by the government and expressly reserved for Tibetan children. The children came from families of middle class farmers, the poor small-time merchants, craftsmen and hired workers. Children went to school between 6 -7 to 12 - 14 years of age. School lasted six hours a day and included two hours of Chinese, one hour of politics, one hour of Tibetan, one hour of arithmetic and one hour of gymnastics and singing. Books and writing materials were provided by the school; uniforms and lunch money were given to 50% by the state and the other half was taken from the grain reserves of the village (*spyi 'bru*). Four hours of manual labour were required a week. The education was based on making the children into future farmers. Teachers are, or were, usually Chinese; only a few Tibetans lecture at these schools.

The schools established by Tibetans were first introduced in Lha-sa in 1963. Only the children of the outlawed classes - rulers, their representatives, the rich families who had possessed large herds, counter-revolutionaries - could attend these schools. Instruction lasted all day long; the first half was spent in hard manual labour like fertilizing the fields or cleaning the toilets; Politics, the Tibetan and Chinese languages, Arithmetic, Singing and Gymnastics were the subjects taught during the second half of the day. The parents of the children had to pay the teachers' salaries as well as for education materials. Children whose parents had fled to India were cared for by the local committee.

Students from the state-run elementary schools were allowed to transfer directly to the intermediate school, while children from the peoples' elementary school were rarely accepted into the middle school unless they had already worked for three years as a land labourer in a commune. There were about six or seven intermediate schools in the whole country.[16] Lha-sa with 300 students, Shigatse with 200, Gyantse with a little over 100 students, Chamdo with 200 students and Nag-chu with 100 students. Intermediate school also lasted about six to eight years and the subjects were: the Chinese script and language, Mathematics, Politics, Chinese History, Tibetan, Military exercises and manual labour. Before 1966 there were many Tibetan instructors at the intermediate schools, but thereafter they were replaced by the Chinese.

The Economy

Although Mao Tse-tung had said in 1952 that the distribution of property had to be initiated by the non-Chinese minorities themselves (Tibet 1968, 44), one year later the Chinese newspaper, *Jen-min Jih-pao*, reported that the land reforms had been started among the minorities following the same basic guidelines as China had (Tibet 1968, 27). Until 1959 Peking had continuously announced that the old system was not to be changed against the will of the Tibetans yet the local cadres began their collectivization everywhere. However, the changing of the whole economic system did not begin in earnest until after 1959.

The Chinese kept the old division of agriculture into three parts while they were transforming the economy. As formerly, one distinguished between farmers with fields (*zhing pa* or *rong pa*) strictly used for crops; shepherds and animal breeders (*'brog pa*) who expansively pursued animal husbandry; and farmers with mixed agricultural practices (*sa ma 'brog* or *yul ma 'brog*) who kept farms in the valleys and herds on the slopes.

The goal of the Chinese economic policies was from the very beginning to establish communes. Step by step the communist party edged its way in that direction.

As was mentioned before, the Chinese officials abolished all taxes in 1959. Those who had been involved in the March 1959 uprising were expropriated and their lands handed over to the poor, who then worked the fields as if they were their own.

The "mutal-aid-teams" (*rogs res tshogs pa*) were a first step toward communalization. There were meetings in the villages at which there were usually some, who, drawn by various promises, supported the establishment of a "mutual-aid-team". Everyone was then requested to make his mark or sign his name to a contract declaring his determination to establish a "mutual aid team" at once. At this stage the farmers were still allowed to live in their own homes and had part of their former land to cultivate. Agricultural implements, however, had to be collectively borrowed from the government; the field work was also collectively carried out. The total harvest was brought in and then divided among the members.

A Tibetan woman, who had been classified by the Chinese as a "liberated serf" and had dedicated herself to her work so that she soon held a leading position in the "Red-flag" commune near Lha-sa, fled to India in 1973 and described her life in the commune (Dhondub Choedon 1978); her report supplements the picture given by Kunzang Paljor.

In the first phase of "democratic reform" in this particular area every person capable of working received a piece of land that required about 9 *khal* (121,5 kg) of seed which meant that c. 16.3 *khal* (220 kg) grain remained after deduction of various taxes per head every year. After the establishment of the commune, the ration of grain was once more reduced to 14 *khal* (189 kg). This was 26 *khal* resp. 28 1/3 *khal* (351 resp. 382,5 kg) less per head than the individual had had before the "liberation". Gold, jewelry, etc. was often sold during this period or was used as a security in order to get a larger piece of land. The black market thrived and that the local authorities prospered is self-evident. Experimental communes had already been set up in Lha-sa, Lhokha and Shigatse in 1962. Each able-bodied person received 12,5 *khal* of grain a year. Since all other necessities like butter, meat, cloth and shoes had to be bought in the commune store, the cash that one earned was often not enough. Debts were taken on that grew from year to year. According to Dhondub Choedon (1978, 35), 14,5 kg of grain were at the disposal of a Tibetan field hand per month. Should he want to buy salt, butter etc., then he had to exchange a part of his grain ration for it. The woman mentioned above also cites a series of cases where lack of an adequate diet had led to the death of some commune members. Many other reports even up into the last few years have told of the deficient nutritional basis.[17]

The yield of the communes was divided as follows according to Kunsang Paljor (1971, 17f):

1. A general grain tax for the fatherland (*rgyal gces spyi 'bru*); this was sent to China.
2. Left-over grain (*'bru lhag spus tshog*), is used to trade for meat, clothes etc. Only insofar as this grain depot is filled can these items be obtained.
3. Payment for the borrowed state-equipment (*son skyin sprod pa*) that is loaned out every spring.
4. Grain for the expansion of the commune (*mi dmangs spyi khang 'dzugs skrun ched 'bru rigs*).

These divisions make up 80% of the harvest. The rest is used to feed the commune members.

Agricultural techniques have been much improved according to Chinese sources (Tibet 1968, 713). P. Aufschnaiter reported, however, that farming methods had not changed at all since 1940 in the Manasarova lake district. Tibetans also point out themselves that much of the so-called success of Chinese agricultural methods is fictitious. A comparison of two reports about the same event may make the situation a little clearer.

The New China News Agency reported from Lha-sa on Jan. 7, 1967, (Tibet 1968, 715f) "The Phari area of Tibet, high up in the Himalayas, trebled its grain output in 1966 and reported a grain surplus for the first time in its history. This is the sixth annual harvest reaped by the Phari people who, in defiance of traditional beliefs and taboos, are pioneering agriculture at 4,200 metres above sea level.... They organized themselves into "mutual-aid-teams" and began to open up the wasteland with knives and other simple tools. With the help of the People's Liberation Army units and the Local Committee, they produced the first sizable harvest in 1961. The annual grain output, at first only a few tons a year, rose to 100 tons in 1965 and 310 tons in 1966".

Kunsang Paljor (1971, 15) writes: "From 1959 on, the Red-Chinese army had forced the people of Phag-ri (Phari in English usage) to grow grain. All this grain, though, was completely unripe and had no kernel (i.e. the grains husks were empty) so that it was comparable to draff (the Brewer's grain); the people of Phag-ri had to eat this from then on. There has never been a more miserable foodstuff, yet the Chinese use it for propoganda!" Similar events have supposedly happened in other regions too.

Animal husbandry was much supported by the Chinese. The number of animals increased by 60% from 1959 to 1965; the herd in any particular village is not allowed to sink under 5% of the former stock. Those shepherds and breeders who took part in the 1959 revolution had everything completely confiscated and the owners of large herds soon came next.

Six to seven families of shepherds made up a "mutual-aid-team". They were permanently settled by the Chinese and because of this there was sometimes the problem of getting enough grazing land for the animals. This resulted in continual protests and unrest on the side of the shepherds. The Chinese then had to assign them to large areas of pasture-land, within which they could wander from meadow to meadow as they had always done before. The shepherds have put up stubborn resistance even up to today against the changes brought by the Chinese, some of them refuse to deliver the full taxes demanded of them. This resistance is favoured by the remoteness of the herding area, and by the fact that the Chinese would be very unwilling to live as administrators or overseers with the shepherds whose way of life is to them even more strange than that of the Tibetan farmers. Each 1000 families of shepherds are bound together as a unit at whose top is a Chinese official. This unit has the right to exchange slaughtered animals with a commune for grain.

The following taxes are to be paid by shepherds:
1. A patriotic shepherd's tax (*rgyal gces 'brog khral*), by which is meant the occasional demand for animals to feed the PLA or to be shipped to China.
2. The delivery of wool, tailhairs, skins and furs in spring and autumn (*ston dpyid gnyis la rtsid pa dang rnga ma pags rigs bcas kyi khral*).
3. The butter and cheese tax which amounted to between 40 and 45% of the total yield.

Fifteen to twenty percent of the wool belonged to the shepherd, the rest had to be delivered up. The basic measurement was the yield of one sheep; for a cow the herdsmen had to deliver an amount three times as much, for a *mdzo mo* (a cross between a *'bri* and a bull) they were to deliver eight times and for a *'bri* five times as much as for one sheep.

The grain obtained by exchange from the agricultural communes is equally divided among working members of the family. The grain ration is lower than that of the field workers because the shepherds enjoy cheese, yoghurt, and butter which is missing from the diets of the farmers today. The diet of the shepherds in general is much better than that of the communal members, but the local mobility of the shepherds is much more limited than that of the communes.

Kunsang Paljor (1971, 27) claims that, until the beginning of the 1970's the Chinese had very little success in instituting their socio-economic plans among the shepherds; their areas have been and still are nests of resistance.

Farmers with mixed agricultural practices (*sa ma 'brog*) have the same taxes to pay from the yields of their fields as the farmers who only grow crops. Double the tax paid by shepherds is levied on their herds. This taxation rate is also used in the hundred county researched in the Gyantse district.

All merchandise was confiscated by the Chinese government from 1959 - 1962. Rich merchants were expropriated without compensation. Small middle-sized traders could continue their businesses but their basic capital was limited to a certain amount which could not be overstepped. After 1962 most of the traders were accepted as employees in the National Trade Organization. In 1970 there were only four free merchants in all of Lha-sa who were allowed to trade. Twenty-five per cent of the income belonged to the merchant (Kunsang Paljor 1971, 28ff).

Several travellers who have recently toured Tibet affirm that a relatively broad variety of goods is sold in the market and in the shops of Lha-sa, though Tibetan refugees claim that most of these items are just for show or for the Chinese cadres, but never available for the common Tibetan worker. If a commoner wants to buy any goods, he has to show a special licence, though the prices are usually high compared with the average wages. Perhaps the situation at the customers' market may have become better during the recent liberalization, though I have no details.

The administrative structure of the counties was re-organised by the Chinese. At the top of each village (*grong*) a Tibetan was named as "head of the assembly" (*tshogs dpon*). He has to pass on the Chinese demands to the Tibetan people and to guarantee their correct implementation. Each village is administered by an assembly of four or five persons: the head, already mentioned, a Chinese official who is in charge of planning, a translator, and one or two Tibetans.

In former days the hundred-county under investigation was an independent unit, directly subordinate to the district governor in Gyantse, but in present times this county belongs to a newly established district with a former neighbouring county as district capital. This district is now managed by the authorities of Shigatse. Thus the researched hundred-county was separated from its former administrative centre and embedded in a totally new one.

SUMMARY

The results of this investigation show that, despite the limited sources, a series of hitherto unknown facts and relationships have come to light. Even if the case study has concentrated on a particular area the trans-regional validity of the results should be recognised.

The original idea was to make a case study in order to avoid false generalizations. But now, it may be admissible to point out the general aspects of the study. The geographical situation is characteristic of many settled areas of Tibet becaue of its low rainfall and high altitude; correspondingly the agricultural possibilities are also typical. The living space, which makes a mixed agriculture necessary, has features that are characteristic of a large part of Tibet. The settlements being divided according to categories of subjects was a wide spread custom, too. Although the interaction between the individual groups exhibited characteristics certainly unique to the researched area, apart from these peculiarities, a system of social structure applicable to wide areas is produced. Observations about the family, system of norms, and stratification presented here are of a general nature. The economy is closely related to the respective interdependencies; the general validity of concrete statements must therefore be strictly limited. Yet the economic structure of the researched hundred-county is an example of the economic systems found in poorer districts of Tibet. Ignoring the figures and numerical ratios, a certain general significance is to be found in the type of economic structure shown here. The manner of structure, made clear here in the example of three villages, characterizes not only broad regions of Tibet in the last decades of independence but also the relationships as formed in the last two or three centuries. Herewith is set at the disposal of Tibetologists, a model of the socio-economic structure of central Tibet, useful for further research in the fields of Tibetan economic and social sciences.

Another question might be if and in what way Buddhist ethics have influenced the shaping of social life. Europeans of the most varied character who visited Tibet from the seventeenth up to the twentieth century have invariably described the Tibetans as being; "kind, gentle, honest, open and cheerful" (Richardson 1962, 10). The minimal amount of aggression in Tibetan society demands an explanation. (In spite of the small amount of aggression there have sometimes been incidents of hardness and brutality.) A comparison was made between the actual behaviour of the persons researched and the generally accepted moral teachings of Mahayana Buddhism; it was found that these precepts had substantial effects even upon the education of small children, not to mention relationships between subjects and authority. A reason for the extraordinary constancy of the Tibetan socio-economic system seems to be in the tendency to repress aggression rather than let it be expressed, under no circumstances to destroy the harmony of the primary group and to allow each person in the group a certain freedom of movement.

Finally the question needs to be answered whether or not the People's Republic of China was in a position to recognize unique features of the economic system in Tibet and include them in their plans for reform. Till now, however, their stubborn clinging to Communist thought patterns has largely prevented the Chinese from seeing the difference between slavery or serfdom and the system of dependency under which Tibetans stood. They looked for an enslaved proletariat where there were only poorer or richer farmers. The basis for a Communist revolution was absent from Tibet. This is also verified by the high percentage of small-tenant farmers and hired workers among the refugees in India. Even the so often cited technological progress has brought hardly any advantage for the Tibetans themselves. Whereas a poor tenant family of the noble estate had formerly received 283 kg of grain a year, a worker today receives about 189 kg grain a year (Dhondub Choedon 1978, 11 and 7), half of which he has to spend on butter, meat, tea and salt. From this grain ration, members of the family who cannot work, the old and sick, have also to be fed. The circumstances of the poor, then, have not improved at all while the majority of the tenants who formerly received between 500 and 600 kg of grain annually per working adult, have a much worse standard of living. Even more disheartening than the undernourishment is, however, the destruction of the social structure and the system of norms, that has led to a cultural and social uprooting of Tibetans. The occupation of Tibet may have brought China more land rich in natural resources, high in agricultural yields and in strategic significance, but for the Tibetans this action has meant poverty, loss of social position and destruction of their values and national identity. The idea of reforming obsolete political and social structures had been formed among progressive Tibetans long before the entry of the Chinese - only the time for ripening was not available.

Many indications, however, let hopes grow that the new politics of the People's Republic of China under Deng Hsiao-ping will allow Tibetans more personal freedom to develop and preserve their own culture. It would be exemplary for the conflicts of this world if these two so different peoples, the Tibetans and the Chinese, could find their way back to a friendly co-existence like the one that they had carefully practised for hundreds of years.

NOTES

To Chapter I

1. Snellgrove/Richardson 1968, 245; a very sympathetic report on dGe-'dun-chos- phel's life was published recently by K. Dhondup (1978, 10 ff).
2. Socio-anthropological explorations among Tibetan speaking populations living in the Himalayan border regions may not replace investigations carried out among the Tibetans themselves, as those settlements exhibit some traits significantly different from the culture of Tibet proper
3. Goldschmidt (1972, 59) ponders on the impact of language exerted on our understanding of human culture. Snellgrove (1966, 208) explains: "Of the many sides of Tibetan studies, it is manifestly the colloquial language which is his medium par excellence. The colloquial language is his only direct means of contact with the people in whom he is interested".
4. König 1966 a; Arensberg 1967, 498-521; Lynd/Lynd 1929/1956; Redfield 1955; Shanin 1971.
5. Cf. the evaluation of Szczepanski 1967, 551-569; König/Schmalzfuss 1972, 21; Langness 1965.
6. For further information vd. Scheuch 1967, 165f; König 1967a, 206; König 1972 a; Gordon 1969; Schrader 1971. 94 ff and 123 ff.
7. This problem is evaluated by several sociologists within König 1972b, 51-167; the researcher's role is discussed by Kluckhohn in König/Schmalzfuss 1972, 97-114.

To Chapter II

1. For further details vide chapter Vii. Economy.
2. Jäschke 1949 renders for one *bre* the measure of four pints.

To Chapter III

1. The structure of the former Tibetan government was described by a few authors: Carrasco 1959, 79ff; Richardson 1962, 18 ff; Goldstein 1971 b; Brauen 1974, 105 ff.
2. Cassinelli/Ekvall 1969, 344 f give a lively scene as to how the subjects exerted a considerable force on the ruling class; further vd. Richardson 1962a, 25. Tucci (1966, 18) refers to folksongs as exhibiting the public opinion; the same was observed by Bell (1928, 171 ff). Taring (1970, 25 and 45 f) gives almost identical information.
3. Johnson 1960, 63ff: "Any partial structure – a type of sub-group, a role, a social norm, or a cultural value — is said to have a function if it contributes to the fulfillment of one or more of the social needs of a social system or sub-system; any partial structure is said to have a dysfunction if it hinders the fulfillment of one or more of these needs".
4. The term *mi ser* was translated by several authors in different ways: Carrasco (1959, 44f) says "tenant, landholders", which corresponds to Brauen (1974, 105) "Untergebener", preferred by myself, Cassinelli/Ekvall (1969, 77ff) gives details about the rights and duties of a *mi ser*. Goldstein renders the term by using the word "serf" that seems to me ambiguous and prejudiced against the Tibetan system of society till now not very well known.
5. Johnson (1960, 205): "The use of forced labor in production has been and is extremely common ... For example, subject peoples have been forced to work on public projects, such as roadbuilding. (Before the Revolution in France this kind of labor-tax, forced upon the home sub-

6. jects, was known as corvée)".
   Rauber-Schweizer (1976, 48) uses the term *mi bog* – apparently a different spelling for *mi bogs* – only in the meaning "human lease; an annual fee paid by a serf to his master or owner for exemption from corvée labour on an estate".
7. For the value of Tibetan coins cf. Brauen 1974, 165 ff.
8. Wössner 1971, 102: "Als Primärgruppe bezeichnete Cooley Gruppen, in denen 1. enge face-to-face Beziehungen vorherrschen und 2. ein Wir-Gefühl vorhanden ist und 3. eine hohe Integration des Einzelnen in der Gruppe vorliegt".
9. Wössner 1971, 239: "Das Ständesystem ist keine so streng gescholossene Gesellschaft wie das Kastensystem. Zwar ist die Zugehörigkeit zu einem Stand im allgemeinen erblich, wird aber doch durch bedeutende Modifikationen gemildert. Eine solche Modifikation ist etwa die Kooptation, d.h. die Zuwahl neuer Mitglieder. Eine weitere Möglichkeit stellt die "Erhebung" in einen höheren Stand dar (...) Ein höherer Status kann auch aufgrund von Heirat erreicht werden".
10. Johnson (1960, 11 n.4): "The culture of a subgroup is sometimes called a subculture. Just as "groups" and "subgroups" are relative to one another, so are "cultures" and "subcultures". A similar opinion is rendered by Wössner (1979,92).
11. In his autobiographical work, the Dalai Lama refers to similar cases, when he says the farmers' property was heritable, might be rented or leased to anybody else as well as the usage of the land could be sold. Though actually the right to use a plot was rarely sold, as every farmer was concerned to hand over the farm without any loss to the next generation (Dalai Lama 1962, 84).
12. The Dalai Lama (1962, 84) states that a subject failing in providing the required taxes and service might get rid of his property, though my informants denied such a possibility. Only the shepherds conceded that a herdsman failing in paying his taxes during a course of several might be ousted.

To Chapter IV

1. Though Stein (1972, 92) denies the existence of a middle class in former Tibet, the reports of Bell (1968, 29ff) and Snellgrove/Richardson (1968, 248 ff) disclose some material suggesting a certain social stratum which might well deserve the name "middle class".
2. For more material on that issue vide Filchner 1933, 378 and Richardson 1962, 16.
3. Kamalaśīla, Bhāvanākrama I (ed. and transl. Tucci 1958 vol. 2, 231): *de bas na sangs rgyas kyi chos thams cad kyi rtsa ba ni snying rje chen po kho na'o //*
   (op.cit. 229) *Thams cad mkhyen pa nyid myur du thob par 'dod pas mdor na snying rje dang / byang chub kyi sems dang / sgrub pa dang gnas 'di gsum la 'bad par bya'o //*
   "The great compassion is the unique root for all the Buddha's qualitites".
   "If one seeks for obtaining soon the all-embracing wisdom (*sarvajñā*), in short, three disciplines should be strived for: compassion, the mind directed towards enlightenment, and realization".
   (This translation does not follow the exact words of Tucci.)
4. Bell (1928, 157), who acted as British representative in Tibet during a period of years, says: "Feudalism is tempered with a strong democratic instinct". Richardson, his countryman, agrees with the latter: "No district official or local landlord, even in a remote area could afford to exceed the customary limits of strictness or exaction, for the ultimate sanction of his authority was popular consent guided by traditional usage" (Snellgrove/Richardson 1968, 259).

To Chapter V

1. For further discussion of the Tibetan family structures vd.: Bell 1928, 175 ff, Hermanns 1949, 229: Aziz 1969, 160; Aziz 1978, 168 ff, Stein 1972, 94ff.
2. Johnson (1960, 155) as well as Wössner (1971, 184) define the "extended family" as consisting of the kinsmen of various generations living together in a common home.
3. Both authors (loc.cit.) explain the "nuclear family" as consisting in the relationship between husband and wife.
4. The fact of polyandry in Tibet is discussed by several authors: Prince Peter of Greece 1963, Bell 1928, 29, 159, 192 ff; Hermans 1949, 164; Carrasco 1959, 32, 47 f. 68 f, 210, 212, 229; Stein 1972, 96 ff; Brauen 1974, 77, 80; for the sociological aspects cf. Johnson 1960, 150, 152, 156; Wössner 1971, 185.
5. Hermans (1949, 229) gives almost identical figures referring to the herdsmen of East Tibet.
6. This custom is also documented for the royal family of Derge by Stein (1972, 106).
7. This was observed by Bell (1928, 157) too; for matrilineal lineages vd. Mühlmann 1964, 221-247.
8. Bell (1928, 156 ff) provides material on this issue and many further references; further vd. Stubel 1958, 52 f.
9. This meditation is fully explained by Tsong-kha-pa in his Lam-rim-chen-mo (Lha-sa print fol. 167a.3 ff). The essential parts out of this passage were translated by my husband and myself. (Dargyay/Dargyay 1979, 118).
10. Bell (1928, 161 f) states that women acted as advisers in political affairs.
11. Bell (1928, 173 f) renders a list of qualities desirable for upper class women.
12. Buddhist morals disapprove "impure conduct" (*mi gtsang ba'i spyod pa*), that means to have extra-marital sexual intercourse with varying partners.
13. Hermanns (1949, 230) agrees with my experience referring to the situation in Amdo: "Die Kinder sind zwar willig und gehorsam. Doch werden erwachsene Söhne auch um Rat gefragt".
14. Bell (1928, 176) describes this particular change in arranging marriages already at the beginning of this century.
15. For Tibetan marriage customs vd.: Bell 1928, 178 ff; Ribbach 1940, 53-117; Stubel 1958, 52; Duncan 1964, 92 ff; Taring 1970, 66-94; Schuh 1973, 295-349.
16. These two different systems were also alluded by Aziz (1969, 160 and 1978, 127).
17. The interdependence between the people observed and the observer is described in a subtle way by Leighton/Kluckhohn 1972. 134, 141, 145; vd. further Mauss 1972, 100.
18. The same was experienced by Bell (1928, 196).
19. As so-far there is little change in bringing up and educating children, I use the present tense in this passage. Cf. also the informations given by Snellgrove/Richardson 1968, 259.
20. Learned scholar-monks used to write down their exhortations for lay people in a condensed form like poems, what became a category of literature by its own.
21. Johnson (1960, 34): "Let us designate as 'ego' any person who is taken as the point of reference in a discussion. (This is a fairly common practice in anthropology, clinical psychology, and sociology.). We shall here use 'ego' to refer to a person in his capacity as occupant of a particular social position".

To Chapter VI

1. Chandra 1971, 908 f: *bsnyung bar 'dugs pa*.

2. There are several issues of this text. At my disposal is a copy published recently by the junior tutor of the present Dalai Lama. This text has the title: *Theg chen gso sbyong gi sdom pa len pa'i cho ga nag 'gros su bkod pa byang chen khang bzang 'dzegs pa'i them skas zhes bya ba bzhugs so.*
3. Bell (1928, 61) describes the day's work of a Tibetan Buddhist.

To Chapter VII

1. The word yak is often used in Western literature for the female animal of the *bos grunniens*. It is, however, only the phonetic transcription of the Tibetan word *g-yag*, which denotes exclusively the male animal. So it is rather peculiar to speak of yak-milk, yak-calves, etc. It is therefore more appropriate to use the correct word for the female *bos grunniens*, i.e. *'bri*, pronounced "dree".
2. Breeding of the *mdzo mo* was impossible, because they gave birth to very vulnerable calves that usually died a few weeks after birth.
3. The worth of the money can only be estimated by comparison. 1 *khal* of butter cost 6 *rdo tshad* in the county; cf. Cassinelli/Ekvall 1969, 377.
4. 1 **ta'o* was equivalent to approximately ¼ *khal* or 3.4 kg.
5. Brauen 1974, 135; Taring 1970, 7; Richardson 1962, 15. The same practice was found to have existed in earlier times, see Stein 1972, 132.
6. The definitions by Goldstein (1971 a, 7) were not verified. The steward of the lower settlement reported that one **rkang* only meant two workers in the upper settlement. However, the dual-tariffed inhabitants of that settlement denied this.
7. One of the stewards, who was hard-working and reliable, was excused for a minor encroachment and urged to stay in his position.
8. A disinherited tenant's son managed to save up a small fortune by hiring himself out and was thereby able to enter the dual-tariffed tax-payers' category.
9. The normal Tibetan cheese (*chu ra*) is not salted; sometimes it is further processed with sugar to make a type of candy.
10. SCD 261 lists several diseases that begin with the syllable *glo*, "lung", but none of them was described as being an animal disease.
11. Similar vaccinations were common in other places also. The family members of someone who came down with smallpox ate small pieces of the infected skin whereupon, after recovering from a few days' sickness, they were for the most part immune. Hermanns (1949, 208 f) reports the same phenomena from Amdo.
12. It has been reported from East Tibet that leather sacks were used instead of churns. The sack filled with milk was kneaded until butter was produced. Sometimes yoghurt was added to the milk.
13. Cf. n.6 (chapter VII); according to that steward's statement it might also be only 28 workers.
14. One tenant reported a field size of 60 *khal*. However, since this person proved to be rather unreliable in all his information, I relied upon the data given by all the other tenants.
15. The amount could no longer be remembered by the questioned person.
16. Richardson (1962, 12) says: "Almost every family in Tibet contributed at least one member to the religious order". Brauen (1974, 98) remarks that exact figures of the number of monks and nuns living in Tibet were not at hand, so that one has to rely upon estimates. According to these, between 10 and 20 per cent of the Tibetan population belonged to the clergy.

To Chapter IX

1. Most publications of this group have no author's name; further it is almost impossible to quote all these small anonymous articles, so I give only a small list of the more important publications. Chang Kuo-hua 1953; Chang Po-chun 1955; Concerning the Question of Tibet 1959; Facts about Tibet 1965; Glimpses about Tibet 1965; Bright Sunshine in Tibet 1968; Grosse Veränderungen in Tibet 1972; Tibet Heute 1974.
2. Gelder/Gelder 1964; Strong 1959; Winnington 1957; Senanayake 1967; Han Suyin 1977.
3. Tibet Under Chinese Communist Rule 1976; Dhondub Choedon 1978; Gompo Tashi Andrugtsang 1973; Hutheesing 1961; Kunsang Paljor 1971; Moraes 1960; Ford 1957.
4. Dawa Norbu 1974; Taring 1970; Tseten Dolkar 1971; Thubten Jigme Norbu 1972.
5. Tibet and the Chinese People's Republic 1960; Ginsburgs/Mathos 1964; Karan 1976.
6. Ginsburgs/Mathos 1964, 7; Tibet 1968, 1 f; Richardson 1962, 179 ff; Shakabpa 1967, 229 f.
7. Dawa Norbu (1974, 134 ff) reports various deportations within the Sa-skya area; on p. 160 ff he refers to imprisonment and torture suffered by some Tibetans.
8. Dawa Norby 1974, 138f and 141 f: "The teachers of the Institute [of National Minorities in Peking] would exclaim: 'What do you backward Tibetans know? Nothing! The Han race is the bravest, cleverest and most able in the world!'" – "During this purge [after Tibetan students had established a theatre group to perform Tibetan opera] the 'criminals' were made to wear paper hats with 'local nationalism' inscribed on them".
9. Tibet 1968, 432: "In its directive, the CCP Tibet Work Committee pointed out that, simultaneously with the suppression of the rebellion staged by the upper strata reactionary clique in Tibet, it was necessary to render positive leadership over the masses in production, to enforce earnestly the policy of 'all who till the land of the rebels will own the crops they cultivate and will not have to pay any rent' to leave no arable land idle, and to strive for a bumper agricultural harvest in the first year following the suppression of the revolt".
10. Tibet 1968, 600; vide also the detailed report on the "present state of religious institutions in Lha-sa" (Tibetan Review XIII, 1, 4 ff).
11. A map of the newly built roads is given by P. Karan (1976, 47); Tibet 1968, 135 reports: "The Chinese People's Liberation Army units stationed in Tibet organized, together with workers of various nationalities, large highway construction teams".
12. He was named Acting Chairman of the Preparatory Committee for the Tibetan Autonomous Region, cf. Tibet 1968, 386.
13. Ginsburgs/Mathos 1964, 182 tells of the bombing of monasteries and killing of monks; op. cit. p. 184: " ... it should be noted, the new regime began by using its monopoly of armed force to deal with the religious establishment a physical blow from which it would be hard put to recover: destruction of monasteries, dispersal of their personnel, arrests, deportations, closures of temples, liquidated in no time part of the Church's nation-wide organization". Also cf. International Commission of Jurists 1960, 14-58.
14. Similar is alluded to in a report from Lha-sa: "More than 60,000 young Tibetans, most of them children of poor peasants and herdsmen, are studying ..." (Tibet 1968, 590); a wide range of details is committed by Kunsang Paljor 1971, 42-48 and by Dhondub Choedon 1978, 33.
15. International Commission of Jurists 1960, 52 presents documents from Gyaldring, Taktse near Lha-sa, and on p. 53 from Ba and Tastang in Amdo; Dawa Norbu 1974, 134 ff tells about the intended sending of his sister to school in China.
16. According to Kunsang Paljor (1971, 48) six schools existed, while Tibet 1968, 590 gives the figure of seven schools.
17. Dhondub Choedon 1978, 36; Tibetan Review VIII, 5, 4 f; Kunsang Paljor 1971, 18 f.

APPENDIX

MEASURES AND WEIGHTS

Most of the Tibetan measures are cubic measures used for measuring grain. Different weights were used for butter, meat and wool. The dictionaries of Tibetan language (Jäschke 1949, SCD, Goldstein 1975) give information on weights and measures to some extent, also some publications focussing on Tibetan economy. These data were compared by me with those delivered by the informants of the researched area. In most points both sources, Western publications and Tibetan informants, agreed with each other.

For further information see:

Roerich/Phuntshok 1952, 47; Surkhang 1966, 18; Cassinelli/Ekvall 1969, 376 f; Brauen 1974, 142.

Cubic Measures

 1 *khal* = 20 *bre*
   = 12 *lu gu (informant's data)
   = about 6,66 *lcag khal* (informant)
   = **ta'o*, also spelled *to ba (is it to be connected with *tog ge* (Goldstein 1975, 476)? (informant)
   = 4 *lcag dung (informant)
   = 4 *'bo* (Roerich/Phuntshok)
   = 2/3 * *ru'i khal* (informant)

Weights

The *khal* is also a weight.
1 *khal* = 80 *spor* = 20 *nya ga* = 5 *rgya ma*

Table of Conversion

The following figures were exclusively based on information given in the forementioned Western publications.

 1*khal* = 13.5 kg (Brauen 1974m 142)
   = 30 lb. = 13.59 kg (Roerich/Phuntshok 1952, 47; SCD 143)
 1 *bre* = 1 pint = 0.55 l.(Cassinelli/Ekvall 1969, 376)
   = 2 pints = 1.1 l.(SCD 897)
   = 4 pints = 2.2 l.(Jäschke 1949, 381)
   = 10 pints = 5.5 l.(Roerich/Phuntshok 1952, 143)

Apparently the *bre* is a measure of great ambiguity, therefore I preferred the *khal* which I think to be equal to 13.5 kg.

TIBETAN MONEY

1 *srang* = 10 *zho* = 100 *kar ma* = 6 2/3 *tram ka*
50 *srang* = 1 *rdo tshad* (Cassinelli/Ekvall 1969, 376)
1 *tram* = 0.15 *srang* = 1.5 *zho* = 15 *kar ma* (Brauen 1974, 165)

Value

In 1920 1 *rdo tshad* = £4 (Bell 1928, 180)
In 1950 one *khal* of grain was about 20 *srang*; in 1958 one *khal* of grain was about 150 *srang*, according to the village headman. Cassinelli/Ekvall (1969, 377) give the prices for some consumer goods. As far as I know this is the only Tibetan price list so-far published, so it seems worthwhile to repeat some figures that might not be too different from the prices in the researched county.

1 *bre* of barley	=	0.7 *srang*
1 *bre* of wheat	=	0.9 *srang*
1 *bre* of rice	=	2 to 2.5 *srang*
1 *rgya ma* of mutton	=	3 srang
1 sheep	=	20 to 30 *srang*
1 lamb	=	5 to 10 *srang*
1 yak	=	350 *srang*
1 *mdzo mo*	=	600 *srang*
1 horse	=	750 to 1500 *srang*

Wages of Craftsmen

In the researched county, a craftsman got 6 or 7 *srang* for a day's work; occasionally up to 10 *srang* was paid. The goldsmith and the painter of sacrificial images earned the highest wages.

In the Sa-skya principality, a farm labourer got only one *srang* a day; most craftsmen got 3 *srang*, the blacksmith 10 *srang*, and the gold and coppersmith earned 10 to 15 *srang*, the best wage paid in this area.

TAX-RECORD OF THE NOBLE ESTATE FOR SHEEP BREEDING

The actual record was written by the former steward of the noble estate as he remembered it. So the exact figures are fictitious but the amount of the several assessments show a reliable idea of the former tax system.

The translation of the Tibetan text:

1. The Shepherd's Bond

The Shepherd Mig-sril from Zas-khud got sheep. The keeping of accounts will start at the fifteenth day of the sixth month of the fire-mouse year; the balancing has to be rendered at the fifteenth of the sixth month of the fire-ox-year.

Without referring to the death-rate – as stated in the basic [tax] book – the shepherd was actually entrusted [with the given number of sheep beneath] :

Rams

24	grown-up "full-mouther" [i.e. an old wether]
24	"six-teether" [i.e. a four year old wether]
24	"four-teether" [i.e. a three year old wether]
24	"two-teether" [i.e. a two year old wether]
24	male *lag ga* [i.e. a one year old wether]
24	male lambs

Ewes

24	grown-up "full-mouther" [i.e. old ewes;]
24	"six-teether" [i.e. four year old ewes;]
24	"four-teether"
24	"two-teether"
24	female *lag-ga*,
24	female lambs.

In total he obtained 288 male and female sheep on the fifteenth day of the sixth month.

2. Record in the Basic Tax Book of the Landlord
[This record is for the second year of accounting]
The above mentioned shepherd has to render the account for the period starting with the 15th day of the 6th month of the fire-ox-year till the 15th day of the 6th month of the earth-tiger-year.
The death-rate: for every dozen, one beast is to be deducted, i.e. 2 male "full-mouthers", 2 "six-teethers", 2 "four-teethers", 2 "two-teethers", 2 *lag ga*, and 2 male lambs; further 2 old female "full-mouthers", 2 female "six-teethers", 2 female "four-teethers", 2 female "two-teethers", 2 female *lag ga*. and 2 ewe lambs.
In total: 24 sheep.
    Meat-assessment: [The shepherd has to deliver]
4 old ewes to the shepherds and their servants doing their job outside [i.e. on the slopes] ;
10 sheep to the monastery as a reward for the pasturage; 4 old ewes to the tenants in Brag-khul as [part of their] wage;
4 old ewes to the settlers of the upper and lower hamlet as [part of their] wages.
2 old ewes to the two stewards of the estate as [a part of their] wages.
    Balance at the end of the year: The newly born lambs have to be added; the death-rate to be taken off, further there are the assessments of meat and sheep-skin.

44	grown-up "full-mouther",
22	"six-teether",
22	"four-teether",
22	"two-teether",
12	male *lag ga*,
32	male lambs [i.e. 50% out of 2/3 of ewes],
30	grown-up female "full-mouther",
22	female "six-teether",
22	female "four-teether",

22   female "two-teether",
22   female *lag ga*,
32   female lambs.
Altogether 304 sheep.

3. *Assessments of Butter and Cheese*:

In the foregoing shepherd's bond [it is recorded that] he has got 96 ewes of more than 2 years of age. Two-thirds of them are expected to bear lambs and produce butter and cheese. For each ewe he has to deliver 4 *nya ga* of butter, i.e. in total 12 *khal* and 16 *nya ga*, and 1 1/3 *bre* of cheese for each ewe, i.e. in total 4 *khal* and 5 *bre*.

    Hitherto he had delivered 12 *khal* of butter and 4 *khal* of cheese, the rest [of the assessments] has still to follow.

GLOSSARY

Arranged according to the Tibetan alphabet.

khral pa	Tax-payer, i.e. owner of land or herds
chang	A kind of beer, produced from barley
dud chung	lit. "Small family", i.e. a tenant living on a rented plot
phyag mdzod	"Treasurer", responsible for the management of a large estate
'bri	Female of the *bos grunniens*, erroneously sometimes called "yak-cow"
ma deb	"Mother-book", i.e. the basic tax-record
ma gsum bu gnyis	"Three ewes, two lambs, a particular system in leasing sheep-herds of sheep
mag pa	A husband who joins the family of his wife, living together in a single household and bearing their family-name
mi bogs	"Man tax" paid to one's landlord, when moving to a different principality
mi ser	Subject, a person subjected to a higher authority
rdzong dpon	District governor
gzhung rgyug khral pa	A subject of the Tibetan government who has to pay taxes (*khral*) to the same institution.
'u lag	Forced service asked by one's landlord

BIBLIOGRAPHY

ARENSBERG C.M., 1967. Die Gemeinde als Objekt und Paradigma. in: KÖNIG 1967b, 498 - 521.
AZIZ, B.N., 1969. The Structure of Tibetan Rural Society. An unpublished M.A. thesis. University of London.
AZIZ, B.N., 1978. *Tibetan Frontier Families - Reflections of Three Generations from D'ing-ri*. New Delhi.
BELL, C., 1928. *The People of Tibet*. Oxford (repr. 1968).
BOLTE, K.M., KAPPE, D., NEIDHARDT, F., 1968. *Soziale Schichtung*. Struktur und Wandel der Gesellschaft, Reihe B der Beiträge zur Sozialkunde Nr. 4. Opladen 2. Aufl.
BRAUEN, M., 1974. *Heinrich Harrers Impressionen aus Tibet*. Innsbruck.
BRIGHT SUNSHINE IN TIBET, 1968. Anon. in: *China Reconstructs* 17, no. 12. Peking.
CARRASCO, P., 1959. *Land and Polity in Tibet*. Seattle.
CASSINELLI, C.W., EKVALL, R.B., 1969. *A Tibetan Principality - the Political System of Sa-skya*. New York.
CHANDRA, L. (ed.), 1970. *Kongtrul's Encyclopaedia of Indo-Tibetan Culture*, pts. 1 - 3. New Delhi.
CHANG, Kuo-hua, 1953. A New Tibet is Arising. *People's China* 10, May 16. Peking.
CHANG, Po-chun., 1955. First Highways to Tibet. *China Reconstructs* 4, no. 5. Peking.
CONCERNING THE QUESTION OF TIBET, 1959. Anon., ed. by Foreign Language Press. Peking.
DALAI LAMA, 1962. *Mein Leben und mein Volk - die Tragödie Tibets*. München / Zürich.
DARGYAY, E.K., 1972. Zur Interpretation der mythischen Urgeschichte in den tibetischen Historikern. *Central Asiatic Journal* XVI, 161 - 177. Wiesbaden.
DARGYAY, E.K., 1978. Grundherr und abhängiger Bauer in Tibet - eine Analyse der Machtverhältnisse, in: *Proceedings of the Csoma de Kőrös Memorial Symposium*, ed. by Louis Ligeti, 65 - 83. Budapest.
DARGYAY, L. / DARGYAY, E.K., 1979. Meditation im tibetischen Buddhismus. *Prana - Jahrbuch für Yoga 1980* ed. by R. Lobo, 118 - 132. München / Bern.
DAWA NORBU, 1974. *Red Star over Tibet*. London.
DHONDUB, C., 1978. *Life in the Red Flag People's Commune*. New Delhi.
DHONDUP, K., 1978. Gedun Chopel: the Man Behind the Legend. *Tibetan Review*, vol XIII, no. 10, 10 - 18
EKVALL, R. B., 1968. *Fields on the Hoof*. New York.
FACTS ABOUT TIBET, 1965. Anon. in: *Peking Review* VIII, no. 38. Peking.
FILCHNER, W., 1933. *Kumbum Dschamba Ling*. Leipzig.
FORD, R.W., 1957. *Captured in Tibet*. London.
GELDER, S. and R., 1964. *The Timely Rain*. London.
GINSBURGS, G, MATHOS M., 1964. *Communist China and Tibet - the First Dozen Years*. The Hague
GLIMPSES ABOUT TIBET., 1965. Anon., in: *Peking Review* VIII, no. 37. Peking.
GOLDSTEIN, M.G., 1964. A Study of *ldab-ldob*. Central Asiatic Journal IX, 123 ff. Wiesbaden.

GOLDSTEIN, M.G., 1971a. Taxation and the Structure of a Tibetan Village. *Central Asiatic Journal* XV, 1 ff. Wiesbaden.
GOLDSTEIN, M.G., 1971b. The Balance between Centralization and Decentralization in the Traditional Tibetan Political System. *Central Asiatic Journal* XV, 170 ff. Wiesbaden.
GOLDSTEIN, M.G., 1975. *Tibetan-English Dictionary of Modern Tibetan*. Kathmandu.
GORDON, L., 1969. *Interviewing - Strategy, Techniques, and Tactics*. Homewood / Georgetown.
GROSSE VERANDERUNGEN IN TIBET, 1972. Anon., ed. by Foreign Language Press. Peking.
HAARH, E., 1969. *The Yar-luṅ Dynasty*. Kopenhagen.
HAN, S., 1977. *Lhasa - The Open City. A Journey to Tibet*. London.
HEDIN, S., 1922. *Tsangpo Lamas Wallfahrt*. 2 vols. Leipzig.
HERMANNS, M., 1949. *Die Nomaden von Tibet*. Wien.
HUTHEESING, G.P., (ed.), 1961. *Tibet Fight for Freedom*. Bombay.
INTERNATIONAL COMMISSION OF JURISTS, 1960. *Tibet and the Chinese People's Republic*. Geneva.
JAHODA, M., DEUTSCH, M., COOK, St.W., 1972. Beobachtungsverfahren. In: KÖNIG 1972b, 77 - 96.
JOHNSON, H.M., 1960. *Sociology: a Systematic Introduction*. New York.
KAMALASILA, 1958. Bhāvanākrama I. In: TUCCI 1958, II, 187 ff.
KARAN, P., 1976. The Changing Face of Tibet. University of Kentucky Press.
KASCHWESKY, R., TSERING, P., 1973. Die Niederschlagung des Empörers von Nyag-rong und andere Reminiszenzen des dPal-sprul Rin-po-che. *Zentralasiatische Studien* VII, 443 - 475. Wiesbaden.
KLUCKHOHN, F., 1972. Die Methode der teilnehmenden Beobachtung. In: KÖNIG 1972b, 97 - 114.
KÖNIG, R. (ed.), 1966a. *Soziologie der Gemeinde*. Kölner Zeitschrift für Soziologie und Sozialpsychologie, Sonderheft 1, Köln 3. Aufl.
KÖNIG, R. (ed.), 1967a. *Soziologie*. Fischer Lexikon. Frankfurt.
KÖNIG, R. (ed.), 1967b. *Handbuch der Empirischen Sozialforschung*. (2 vols.) 1 vol. Stuttgart.
KÖNIG, R. (ed.), 1972a. *Das Interview. Formen, Technik, Auswertung*. Praktische Sozialforschung 1, Köln 7. Aufl.
KÖNIG, R. (ed.), 1972b. *Beobachtung und Experiment in der Sozialforschung*. Praktische Sozialforschung 2, Koln 8. Aufl.
KÖNIG, R., SCHMALZFUSS, A. (eds.), 1972. *Kulturanthropologie*. Düsseldorf.
KUNSANG P., 1971. *Tibet - the Undying Flame*. (in Tibetan). Dharamsala.
LANGNESS, L.L., 1965. *The Life History in Anthropological Science*. New York.
LEIGHTON, D., KLUCKHOHN, C., 1972. Wie wird man zum Navajo: Die ersten sechs Lebensjahre. In: KÖNIG & SCHMALZFUSS 1972, 129 - 155.
LEVI–STRAUSS, C., 1978. *Struktural Anthropologie* I. Frankfurt.
LUDWAR, G., 1975. *Die Sozialisation Tibetischer Kinder im soziokulturellen Wandel*. Wiesbaden.
LYND, R.S., LYND, H.M., 1929, 1956, *Middletown. A Study in American Culture*. New York.
MANN, L., 1972. *Sozialpsychologie*. Basel.
MORAES, F., 1960. *The Revolt in Tibet*. Delhi.
MÜHLMANN, W.E., 1964. *Rassen, Ethnien, Kulturen. Moderne Ethnologie*. Neuwied / Berlin.
MYRDAL, G., 1969. *Objectivity in Social Research*. New York.
NGAPO, N.J. (et. al.), 1981. *Tibet*. Shanghai.
OPPITZ, M., 1975. *Notwendige Beziehungen*. Abriss der strukturalen Anthropologie. Frankfurt.

PATTERSON, G., 1973. The Long Way Home. *Far Eastern Economic Review* vol. 80, no. 16, 29 - 30. Hongkong.
PEISSEL, M., 1973. *Die Chinesen sind da*! Der Freiheitskampf der Khambas. Wien.
PETECH, L., 1977. *The Kingdom of Ladakh 950-1842 A.D.*. Rome.
PETER OF GREECE, Prince , 1963. *A Study of Polyandry*. The Hague.
RAUBER-SCHWEIZER, H., 1976. *Der Schmied und sein Handwerk im traditionellen Tibet.* Rikon.
REDFIELD, R., 1955. *The Little Community*. Uppsala / Stockholm.
REDFIELD, R., 1956. *Peasant Society and Culture*. Chicago.
RIBBACH, S.H., 1940. *Drogpa Namgyal - ein Tibeterleben*. München.
RICHARDSON, H.E., 1962. *Tibet and Its History*. London.
RICHARDSON, H.E., 1977. The Dharma that Came Down from Heaven: A Tun-huang Fragment. In: *Buddhist Thought and Asian Civilization*, 217 - 229. Emeryville.
ROERICH, G.N., PHUNTSOK, Tse-trung Lopsang, 1957. *Textbook of Colloquial Tibetan*. Dialect of Central Tibet. Government of West Bengal. Calcutta.
SCD = Das, S.C., 1960. *A Tibetan-English Dictionary with Sanskrit Synonyms*. Calcutta 1902, repr. Alipore.
SCHEUCH, E.K., 1967. Das Interview in der Sozialforschung. In: KÖNIG 1967b, 136 - 196 and 707 - 715.
SCHRADER, A., 1971. *Einführung in die empirische Sozialforschung*. Stuttgart / Berlin / Köln / Mainz.
SCHUH, D., 1973. Die Darlegung des tibetischen Enzyklopädisten Kong-sprul blo-gros-mtha'-yas über ost-tibetische Hochzeitsbräuche. *Serta Tibeto-Mongolica*, 295 - 349. Wiesbaden.
SENANAYAKE, R.D., 1967. *Inside Story of Tibet*. Colombo.
SHAKABPA, Tsepon W.D., 1967. *Tibet. A Political History*. New Haven / London.
SHANIN, T., 1971. *Peasants and Peasant Societies*. Harmondsworth.
SMITH, E., 1970. Introduction to Kongtrul's Encyclopaedia . . . In: CHANDRA 1970.
SNELLGROVE, D.L., 1966. For a Sociology of Tibetan Speaking Regions. *Central Asiatic Journal* XI, 199 - 219. Wiesbaden.
SNELLGROVE, D., RICHARDSON, H.E., 1968. *A Cultural History of Tibet*. London.
STEIN, R.A., 1972. *Tibetan Civilization*. London.
STRONG, A.L., 1959. *Tibetan Interviews*. Foreign Language Press. Peking.
STUBEL, H., 1958. *The Mewu Fantzu*. A Tibetan Tribe of Kansu. Behaviour Science Translations. New Haven.
SURKHANG, W., 1966. Tax Measurement and Lag 'don Tax. *Bulletin of Tibetology* III, 1, 15 - 28. Gangtok.
SZCZEPANSKI, J., 1967. Die biographische Methode. In: KÖNIG 1967b.
TARING, R.D. 1970. *Daughter of Tibet*. London.
THUBTEN J. NORBU, TURNBULL, C.M., 1972. *Tibet - Its History, Religion and People*. Harmondsworth.
TIBET 1950-1967. 1968. Ed. by Union Research Institute. Hong Kong.
TIBET HEUTE, 1974. Anon., ed. by Foreign Language Press. Peking.
TIBET UNDER CHINESE COMMUNIST RULE, 1976. A Compilation of Refugee Statements 1958 - 1975. Ed. by Information and Publicity Office of H.H. the Dalai Lama. New Delhi.
TIBETAN REVIEW, 1965. The only monthly publication of news, commentary, book reviews and articles on all aspects of Tibet. Ed. by Tsering Wangyal. New Delhi.
TSETEN D., 1971. *Girl from Tibet*. Ed. by John Windsor. Chicago.

TSEWANG, P., 1968. *Tibet im Jahre des Drachens.* (A Novel.) Freiburg.
TUCCI, G., 1941. *Indo-Tibetica.* Rome.
TUCCI, G., 1958. *Minor Buddhist Texts.* Rome.
TUCCI, G., 1966. *Tibetan Folk-Songs from Gyantse and Western Tibet.* 2nd. ed. Ascona.
TUCCI, G., 1973. *Transhimalaya.* New Delhi / London.
VOSTRIKOV, A.I., 1970. *Tibetan Historical Literature.* Calcutta.
WINNINGTON, A., 1957. *Tibet.*
WÖSSNER, J., 1971. *Soziologie. Einführung und Grundlagen.* Wien.
WYLIE, T., 1959. A Standard System of Tibetan Transcription. *Harvard Journal of Asiatic Studies* 22, 261 - 267.

MAPS AND PLANS

KEY TO MAPS

▨	Houses of government tax-payers
▦	Houses of the monastery's tax-payers and tenants, temples and monks' lodgings
▪	Houses of the nobleman's tax-payers and tenants, nobleman's mansion
▨	Houses of dual-tariffed subjects
☰	Houses of the *dud chung*, i.e. sharecroppers and hired workers
≋	Lake
～	River
━	Road from India to Gyantse

A – G	The houses of the seven families who were tax-payers and subjects of the Tibetan government
H	House of the hail-protector
I	Temples
J	Lodgings of former monks
K	Guest-house of the nobleman's estate
L	Guest-house of the Tibetan government
M	Mansion of the monastery's estate
N	Hermitage
O	Temple of Amitāyus
P	House of a hail-protector
Q	Corral with herdsmen's house
R	Nobleman's mansion
S	Park with pavilion belonging to the nobleman's mansion

KEY TO PLANS

A	Windows of different shapes	3	Closet for producing alcoholic drink
B	Stairs to the upper floor	4	Kitchen
C	Door	5	Guest-room
D	Pillar	6	Store-room
E	Girder	7	Chapel
1	Entrance	8	Lavatory
2	Hall with a square aperture in the ceiling		

Map 1. *Village of Government Tax-Payers.*

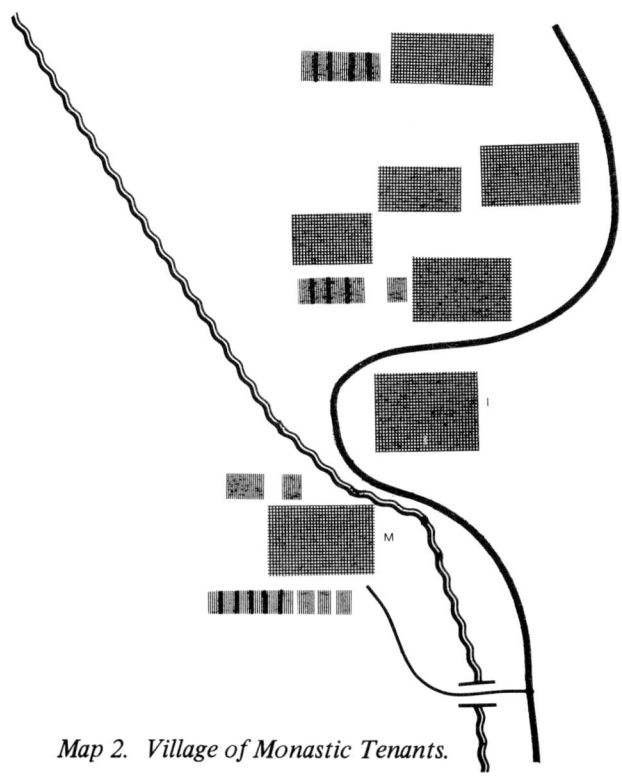

Map 2. Village of Monastic Tenants.

Map 3. Village of the Nobleman's Tenants.

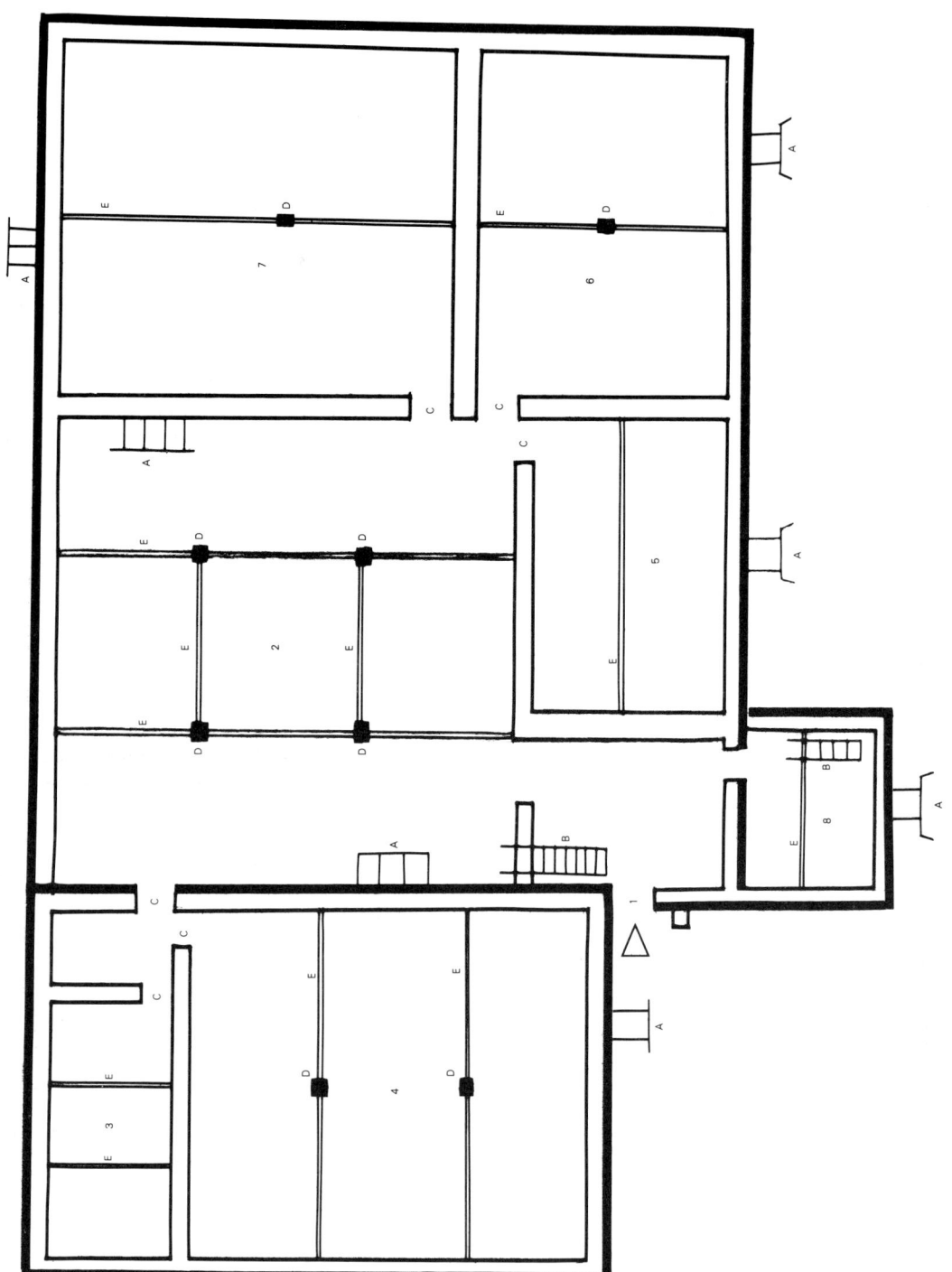

Plan 1. House of a Government Tax-payer (Main floor).

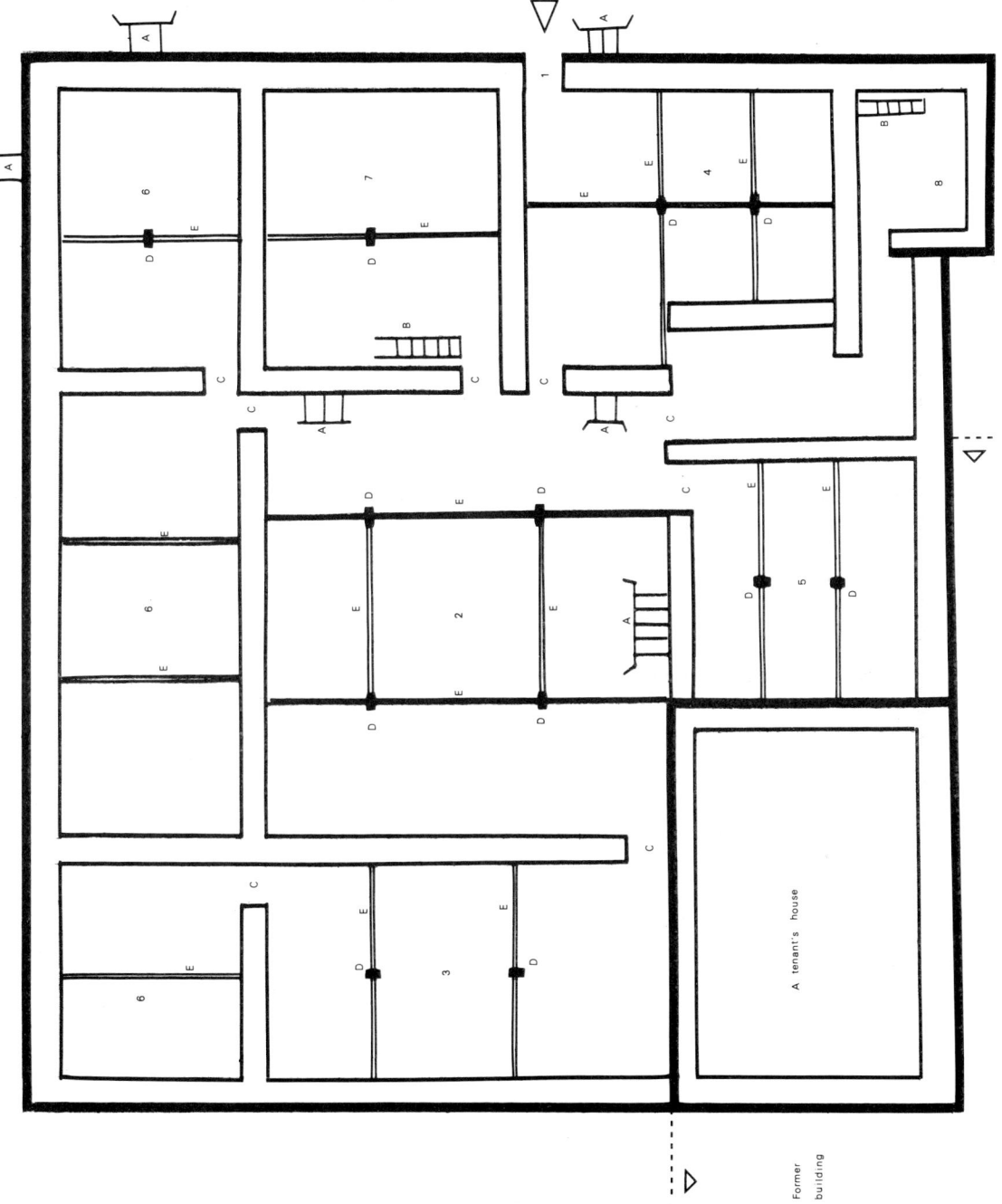

Plan 2. *House of a Government Tax-payer.*